Corn Meal · Corn Flour · Roasted

Kasha · Potato Flour · Potato

Starch · Quinoa · White Rice ·

THE
Gloriously
Gluten-Free
Cookbook

Arborio Rice · Jasmine Rice ·

Brown Rice Flour · White Rice

Flour · Lentils · Teff · Sorghum

• Corn Meal • Corn Flour • Roasted Kasha • Po

Brown Rice • Arborio Rice • Jasmine Rice • Br

Sorghum Flour • Tapioca Starch • Tapioca Flou

Amaranth • Arrowroot • Bean Flours • Buckwhe

Flour • Roasted Kasha • Potato Flour • Potato S

Rice • Jasmine Rice • Brown Rice Flour • White

Starch • Tapioca Flour • Guar Gum • Xanthan

• Bean Flours • Buckwheat • Coconut Flour • C

THE Gloriously Gluten-Free Cookbook

SPICING UP LIFE WITH ITALIAN, ASIAN, AND MEXICAN RECIPES

VANESSA MALTIN

WILEY

JOHN WILEY & SONS, INC.

For general information on our other products and services or for technical support, please contact our Customer Care Department within the United States at (800) 762-2974, outside the United States at (317) 572-3993 or fax (317) 572-4002.

Wiley also publishes its books in a variety of electronic formats. Some content that appears in print may not be available in electronic books. For more information about Wiley products, visit our web site at www.wiley.com.

INTERIOR BOOK DESIGN BY DEBORAH KERNER

Library of Congress Cataloging-in-Publication Data:

Maltin, Vanessa.

The gloriously gluten-free cookbook: spicing up life with Italian, Asian, and Mexican recipes / Vanessa Maitin.

    p. cm.

Includes index.

ISBN 978-0-470-44088-9 (pbk.)

1. Gluten-free diet–Recipes. 2. Cookery, International. I. Title.

RM237.86.M357 2010

641.5'638–dc22

2009009687

Printed in the United States of America

10 9 8 7 6 5 4 3 2

To *Mom, Dad, Stacey, and Eric.* THANK YOU FOR YOUR CONSTANT LOVE AND SUPPORT AND FOR ALWAYS BEING MY GREATEST FANS.

TO ALL THE DOCTORS, CHEFS, AND PATIENTS I'VE WORKED WITH OVER THE LAST SEVERAL YEARS. YOUR PASSION, MOTIVATION, AND DEDICATION ARE MY INSPIRATION FOR EACH AND EVERY RECIPE IN THIS BOOK.

IN LOVING MEMORY OF LELA MAE BEACH, THE GREATEST COOK AND GRANDMOTHER A GIRL COULD EVER KNOW.

Contents

FOREWORD

No one wants to be known as "the sick girl," especially not in television news. We all want to be known for our journalistic prowess, our stunning articulation, or our profound insight into all things newsworthy! But pretty quickly you realize the incredible podium you have in front of millions of people every day, and that ego goes right out the door. It's been interesting sharing some of my health woes on the air. The response has been incredible—but now, I'd like to tell the rest of the story. I share it with you in hopes of shedding more much-needed light on this complicated disease and, of course, because Vanessa asked me to!

When I first got into television news, I dreamed of a career that would include covering the type of stories that would have an impact on people and change their lives. Thirteen years later, I know how rare those types of stories are to find. The Oklahoma City bombing, the Columbine High School massacre, September 11th, the Columbia space shuttle disaster, the Iraq War, the capture of Saddam Hussein, the Southeast Asian tsunami, Hurricane Katrina, the Virginia Tech shootings—all incredible news stories the world will not soon forget. But who would have thought that, of all the stories I've told on the air or covered in the field, the one that has changed the most lives is a story that I never thought I'd have to tell. It is personal, terrifying, and triumphant.

I'd always been told I had a nervous stomach. Nervous to the point of getting physically sick every time I was "stressed out." But I never *felt* stressed out; in fact, I have always thrived in high-pressure situations. It didn't really make sense to me, so I started "the tests." The colonoscopies, the endoscopies, the MRIs, the infinite blood tests, the allergy tests, the cancer tests. . . . I've had them all and they all came back normal. Hence the diagnosis: nervous stomach. A few doctors went so far as to say Irritable Bowel Syndrome (IBS).

That was college: journalism school at the University of Maryland. Then came grad school. More pressure, more work, more expectations . . . more stomachaches. No diagnosis. Press on to my first TV job. I landed the morning and noon anchor position for NBC in Wichita Falls, Texas. It didn't matter to me one bit that it was market 139, I needed experience under my belt. I had married my college sweetheart, Matt, during graduate school, but now that I was in the throes of TV Land, he was the one who always seemed to get the short end of the stick. When I was off the air, I was either complaining of a stomachache or I was completely exhausted. Even my new social life as the wife of an Air Force fighter pilot was a little bizarre. We would have to drive separate cars to parties or dinners with friends because I never knew how long I would last. I felt bad making Matt leave with me because my stomach hurt so much.

Still, the doctors were at a loss. "Nothing a little Pepto-Bismol won't cure" . . . and oh yeah, "try to relax." So—press on. Matt and I decided it would be a good time to start a family. I got pregnant immediately and we were thrilled. I kept it a secret from the viewers until finally, there was no denying it: I was getting quite a baby bump and pretty round in the face too. I announced our pending little bundle live on the air with a special series on pregnancy. We had waited nearly seven months to share our news with the very warm and interested public. Two weeks later, we lost the baby. No explanation except "placental demise." I was so far along that I was taken to the hospital immediately to have the baby. It was the first time I saw my husband cry. It was a girl. Our hearts grieve to this day.

My next job came as the main evening anchor for CBS in Colorado Springs, Colorado. Great place, great job, great friends. But it was here that I almost died. After a hike up Pikes Peak one day, I pulled a calf muscle . . . or so I thought. When the pain didn't go away for about a week, I ended up in the emergency room at the Air Force Academy. Thank God the ER doc had the smarts to do an ultrasound. He found a blood clot in my right leg. I had no idea what that was and was ready to press on after he gave me some pills or something, but it was nowhere near that simple. He immediately admitted me to the hospital. After three months, two hospitals, a spinal tap, and numerous unsuccessful attempts to keep the clot from moving up my leg, one final procedure accidentally thrust the clot into my artery. The next thing I knew, I was on a flight to the Mayo Clinic in Rochester, Minnesota. I now had what is called an arterial occlusion. I needed surgery fast. I could no longer walk. I had no feeling in my toes and the pulse in my foot was disappearing. The doctors told me that without surgery, I would be able to walk two city blocks and then I'd have to rest. I would be handicapped for life. I was twenty-nine years old.

Once again, I was very sick, but I had no diagnosis. Not one of the twenty-five physicians on my team at the Mayo could figure out how or why I had this life-threatening blood clot. They did mention something that would later become paramount in my medical history: a consistently positive antinuclear antibody (ANA). It meant I had some sort of autoimmune disease, but no one knew which one. Finally, they told me I had lupus. But since I didn't have any joint pain or swelling or skin rashes, I felt like they were just trying to get a diagnosis no matter how inaccurate it was.

After the bypass surgery, my leg got stronger and stronger. To this day, I have never had another clot and have very little trouble with my leg. Sadly though, my dream of becoming a leg model will apparently never come true because of the five-and-a-half-inch scar on the back of my leg!

Our true dream to have a baby was also in jeopardy. According to one very cruel, egotistical, uninformed, vascular-medicine physician, we were told shortly after the bypass we would not be able to have children. He said my veins would never be able to support the stresses of a pregnancy. Well, three years later, we had a beautiful, healthy boy named Riley. Thanks to two injections a day of a blood thinner called Lovenox, I got pregnant and this time had no troubles. In our minds, it was a miracle drug for a miracle little boy.

Professionally, things had progressed well, too. I had moved into the Denver market as an anchor/reporter for the NBC station. At the end of my three-year contract, I was offered a job at CNN. I was ecstatic! I would be doing live, breaking news at the world's largest news network. It wasn't long before I was being flown from Atlanta to New York to anchor the shows broadcast from our bureau. I have never been so excited. Until they asked me and my family to move to New York permanently to continue doing the morning and prime-time shows.

We moved into an apartment in the city and began our lives as a family in the Northeast. Unfortunately, the condition of my stomach had simultaneously deteriorated to a new low. I was going to the bathroom five to eight times an hour . . . God knows how many times a day. I was losing weight and had very little energy. Stress—I thought. A new job, relocating to New York, lots of pressure. But when I was barely able to make it through the first hour of the three-hour morning show I was doing at the time, I knew I had to go through more tests. This couldn't possibly be stress or IBS.

Five months later, we bought a home in Summit, New Jersey, about eighteen miles from the city. After fifteen years of dealing with major stomach problems and letting them completely dictate my life, I saw a new internist who took one look at me and said, "You have Celiac Disease." I will never forget it. He didn't even examine me, he just listened to my symptoms and my story, and said the four words that would change my life forever.

I did the blood test to be certain; I followed up with the endoscopy, and yes, indeed, it was true. I had Celiac Disease.

The diet was overwhelming at first. I couldn't believe how many things I would have to stop eating . . . forever. But for me, the thing that scared me the most was my future health. How would I be at sixty years old? At seventy?

As quickly as I started asking myself those questions I stopped. I knew I would have to take one day at a time and do the best I could to learn about this disease and keep myself healthy. That's exactly what I did. Especially because I knew Celiac was genetic, and that meant our sweet Riley could get it. I started watching him like a hawk: his eating habits, his bathroom habits, his energy level—everything. Right before kindergarten we had him tested. Sure enough, it was positive. Surprisingly, I wasn't upset. I was actually so thankful that I knew what to look for so he could be diagnosed at an early age.

Riley is a champion of the gluten-free diet. I could not be more proud of the way he handles it. In fact, he is the main reason I got involved with the National Foundation for Celiac Awareness and with Vanessa Maltin. I needed to be doing more to help people get diagnosed, to help people feel better. When Vanessa told me that ninety-five percent of people with Celiac are undiagnosed, I thought I would be able to use my voice as a journalist and the morning anchor of *CNN Newsroom* to get the word out. She asked me to become the national spokesperson and I happily accepted!

These days, eating gluten-free is truly the least of my worries.

Now it's more about changing diapers . . . and not my own! God has graced us with a new addition to our family by the name of Owen. He is our beautiful baby boy who came to us through the miracle of surrogacy. We felt we needed to go this route because of my Celiac Disease. Unfortunately, I had had very little improvement since going on the diet nearly four years earlier, and I just didn't feel like my body would be able to support and nourish a baby growing in my tummy. Combine that with my blood clot and late-term pregnancy loss . . . and the doctors agreed.

Today we couldn't possibly feel luckier or more blessed. Our boys are thriving and have already become inseparable. As for me, I'm not giving up on making myself better. I do more and more cooking in my own kitchen to ensure gluten-free food safety and really don't know where I'd be without Vanessa's books! I am thrilled to have been a guinea pig on some of these recipes. They are easy, fast, and most important, full of flavor. I always get a kick out of throwing dinner parties and whipping up something very impressive that contains no trace of gluten. When I tell my guests during dessert that the whole meal was gluten-free, they are always shocked. So, take this book with you everywhere you go. Read it, learn from it, and enjoy life with great-tasting food. It's all possible . . . even as a Celiac!

Good luck and Godspeed.

—Heidi Collins
FORMER *CNN Newsroom* ANCHOR

Doctor's Note

Opening a new cookbook is always an exciting adventure to me. I am often amazed by the author's original ways of mixing and matching ordinary ingredients to create new flavors and dishes full of color and texture. But maybe more importantly, I see a cookbook as an opportunity to create special moments in the midst of our busy "fast food" daily lives: the pleasure of choosing aromatic herbs and fresh ingredients, the fun of preparing and sampling new dishes, the joy of gathering around the table with loved ones, the pride of receiving those well-deserved compliments for a home-made dish, and the reassurance of making healthier food choices. For the many people with Celiac Disease, there is another dimension to cooking the right kind of food: it is therapeutic in the medical sense of the term.

Celiac Disease is an autoimmune disorder of the small bowel, whose lining gets damaged after it is exposed to gluten-containing food. This in turn leads to symptoms of malabsorption with diarrhea, cramping, bloating, weight loss, failure to thrive, and nutrient deficiencies. Untreated Celiac Disease can also cause neurological disorders, skin and joint disease, osteoporosis, and infertility and has been associated with an increased risk of certain cancers.

The only treatment for Celiac Disease at this point is a strict, lifelong gluten-free diet. Gluten is the storage protein of wheat, rye, and barley, but is also present in many prepared foods in the form of emulsifiers or stabilizers. Hence, following a gluten-free diet can be a hard task to achieve when eating prepared food or ordering restaurants meals. The Celiac must become an amateur chemist to read labels; a detective to find gluten-free products; and a model of patience to repeatedly explain to waiters the importance of avoiding any gluten in the making of a meal.

Although there have recently been an increasing number of vendors and restaurants offering gluten-free foods, the choices are often limited, the taste can be marginal, the cost high, and there is sometimes a lingering anxiety regarding cross-contamination when eating out. So it is not surprising that one of the first concerns a person with a recent diagnosis of Celiac Disease expresses is how little good food is left to enjoy once gluten is eliminated from the diet. And the logical consequences of that: how much social life is affected when it's often impossible to share regular meals with others; how difficult it is going to be to maintain a gluten-free diet over time.

A gluten-free diet often becomes synonymous with a joy-free, taste-free, and entertainment-free life. Fortunately, it doesn't have to be that way. Getting inspired by a cookbook and making your own meals will not only give you all the emotional joys of cooking, but will also give you control of the ingredients you are using; and for the person with Celiac Disease, this is crucial for following the right therapeutic diet and gaining peace of mind.

Vanessa Maltin's new cookbook takes it a step further: it actually helps you discover the joys of a gluten-free diet instead of focusing on its restrictions. This book is full of fun recipes, with a whole range of complexity, flavors, and taste, sure to please not only the Celiac patient but also the surrounding family members and friends. In that regard, this cookbook achieves the ultimate goal of a good gluten-free diet: to allow people to enjoy a wide variety of tasty, healthy food and to maintain a full social life. And as any physician will tell you, these are the keys to emotional well-being, an essential quality for anyone with Celiac Disease following a lifelong gluten-free diet.

Best of luck!

—Aline Charabaty, MD
GEORGETOWN UNIVERSITY HOSPITAL
DEPARTMENT OF GASTROENTEROLOGY

ACKNOWLEDGMENTS

Writing this cookbook was the greatest and most wonderful challenge of my life, and I couldn't have done it without the help of several amazing people. I am forever grateful to Eric Weisbrod and Stefanie Kleinman, not only for being the best taste-testers and moral supporters a cookbook author could hope for, but also for constantly helping me chop vegetables, grate carrots, peel potatoes, and carry my groceries in hopes of protecting my injured right hand. When I went through five hand surgeries, these two made sure that I didn't miss a deadline and that I always had a working right hand in the kitchen.

I am eternally thankful for the love, support, and constant encouragement from my parents and sister. Thank you, Dad, for always being one hundred percent honest with me and never letting a recipe pass as just "okay." Because of your fantastic palate, each and every recipe in this book is absolutely amazing.

Thank you to the fantastic chefs who helped make this book possible—Keith Brunell of Maggiano's Little Italy, Edgar Steele of Café Atlantico, and Katie Chin of Thai Kitchen, the author of *Everyday Chinese Cooking*. It is their dedication to cooking gluten-free food that inspired me to write this book and find the motivation to teach everyone on a gluten-free diet how to make these delicious meals at home.

Thank you to Dr. Aline Charabaty of Georgetown University Hospital. She is the greatest gastroenterologist I've ever met and is truly a wonderful human being. Thank you for being a true friend, as well as my doctor, and for always knowing the answers to my medical questions.

Thank you to the National Foundation for Celiac Awareness for inspiring me to try to help people around the world with Celiac Disease live the most delicious lifestyle possible.

Thank you to all the vendors who sent me bundles of products to use in testing recipes, including Bob's Red Mill, Thai Kitchen, Anheuser-Busch, Pamela's Products, and the Brazilian Cheese Bread Company. I am forever grateful to you for helping me find the best ingredients on the market.

I owe a very, very special thank you to Heidi Collins. She is a phenomenal news anchor, a remarkable woman, and a true friend. Every morning I turn on *CNN Newsroom* and I am inspired by her ability to take on the world's most influential personalities and translate what they have to say into information all of us can use. It is largely because of Heidi's commitment to raising awareness of Celiac Disease that gluten-free food is becoming mainstream. Thank you to Heidi for her tremendous work on a national level, but also for taking the time to be a major part of this book. Her entire family helped me test recipes, and even their new puppy, Fin, gave me a paws-up!

Thank you to Ellen Wilcox for letting me invade her gorgeous kitchen and to her daughter Amber for always sharing a smile. Thank you to Heather Rubacky, the best intern ever, who was always willing to lend a helping hand.

Thank you to my wonderful agent, Erin Malone, for her guidance and to my wonderful editor at Wiley, Justin Schwartz. I'll never forget the Birdbath Bakery day. Who knows? Maybe someday they'll make gluten-free food! Thank you to the book's designer, Deborah Kerner, and the copyeditor, Helen Chin.

Thank you to the best friends, taste-testers, and Celiac advocates ever: Thelma Rodin-DeSilva, Julie Neimark, Allison Goldstein, Jennifer Neidenberg, Zach Larnard, J. David Grossman, Jordan Gary, Dr. Mustafa Haque, Dr. Mark Abbruzzese, Andrew Itzkowtiz, Julie Luse, Carolyn Lynch McKinley, Emily Freedner, Lauren Pike, and Manny Haider.

And, finally, thank you to my mom. This is going to sound strange, but thank you for having Celiac Disease and for passing it on to me. I remember the day I was diagnosed, and I'll never forget the look on your face when Dr. Surowitz told me I had it. You cried more than I did because you were so sad you had given it to me. But just take a moment and look at us now. Just a few short years after diagnosis, you and I are both healthy. We're not living in the bathroom, we cook and eat delicious food, and most important, we're happy. We've learned to make gluten-free food that even Dad will eat, and well—if Dad says it's good, then this book is definitely worth reading!

—V. M.

Corn Meal · Corn Flour · Roasted
Kasha · Potato Flour · Potato
Starch · Quinoa · White Rice ·

THE
Gloriously
Gluten-Free
Cookbook

Arborio Rice · Jasmine Rice ·
Brown Rice Flour · White Rice
Flour · Lentils · Teff · Sorghum

INTRODUCTION

Gluten-free food. Yuck! That's what I thought for the first few years I was on a gluten-free diet. The only options were bread that tasted like sawdust, pasta that should have been called paste, and cookies and brownies with a texture more like crumbling plaster than a delectable dessert.

With so few options, why would anyone want to eat gluten-free food? To cure chronic diarrhea, of course!

For the three million Americans with Celiac Disease, gluten-free is the only option. There are no drugs or surgeries to cure this autoimmune digestive disease, and left untreated, Celiac Disease can lead to a host of complications, including cancers, osteoporosis, infertility and pregnancy complications, malnourishment, and other autoimmune diseases. Diagnosis rates have skyrocketed among high-risk patients, largely because of increased awareness efforts.

The only treatment is a lifelong gluten-free diet, avoiding all forms of wheat, barley, and rye. This means Celiac Disease is all about the food you eat.

For the first twenty-one years of my life, I enjoyed the same tasty foods that most people eat. Pizza, pasta, and sandwiches were a large part of my diet, as was beer. Little did I know, these foods were the reason I endured two decades of passing gas at all the most inappropriate moments, diarrhea with no warning, and debilitating migraine headaches. We're talking about headaches so painful that I couldn't stand light, noise, or touch. No medications seemed to work, so I resorted to taking intravenous steroids on a daily basis and had to walk around with an IV attached to my arm. I didn't think it was so bad until my sorority formal.

Just close your eyes and imagine a twenty-one-year-old college junior in a beautiful pink satin floor-length dress, with her hair all done up. It's a beautiful image of me. Almost like a princess. Now, add in a portable IV machine and a bag of IV fluid. . . . Kind of ruins the picture, right?

Thank goodness after twenty-one years of being sick, I was finally diagnosed with Celiac Disease.

At first, I couldn't understand how ingredients as seemingly innocuous as wheat, barley, and rye could cause all my medical problems. After all, grains are supposed to be good for you! And gluten is everywhere.

After receiving my Celiac diagnosis I headed to the grocery store in search of gluten-free alternatives. I purchased as many products labeled "gluten-free" as I could find and rushed home to try them. I was praying that each food would taste better than the last and that I would find my new gluten-free diet both easy to manage and delicious at the same time.

Much to my dismay, I ended up eating exactly one bite of each product before tossing it into the trash can. I was horrified by how bad everything tasted, and I couldn't believe I had just spent over two hundred dollars on food that was practically inedible.

I visited several restaurants in the Washington, D.C., area and found that most chefs gave me blank stares when I tried to explain to them that I couldn't eat gluten. My favorite Celiac moment was when I asked a chef to replace pasta with rice and he responded with, "Would you like whole wheat pasta instead?"

At breakfast I would ask for potatoes or tomatoes instead of toast and the chefs would say, "How about an English muffin or bagel?"

No one seemed to get it! I just didn't understand how chefs could cook food every day for hundreds of people and not know what was in it!

Thus began my quest to become a skilled gluten-free chef and to teach everyone on a gluten-free diet how to make delicious food, too.

I have always loved food. Some of my favorite memories are of helping my mom and grandma in the kitchen when I was a little girl. By the time I was five years old I had learned to churn butter the old-fashioned way, pick herbs and vegetables from the garden, and choose the freshest meats at the grocery store. I was that little kid who told the other shoppers how to pick a tomato and to knock on the watermelon to determine if it was ripe.

Even with my Celiac diagnosis, like anyone else, I still needed to eat a diverse array of foods to stay healthy, and I wanted them to be flavorful to the point of making my mouth water. I wanted creamy risotto with seared scallops, heaping plates of pasta with garden-fresh vegetables, dinner rolls with a crispy crust smothered in butter and garlic, enchiladas with a spicy kick, sushi, pad Thai, and, especially, decadent chocolate cake with a fudgy frosting and fresh raspberries.

I needed these foods not only to quench my palate, but also to convince myself that even with a disease, I was still normal. What is normal? Normal to me is being able to eat at restaurants, cook for my family and friends, and enjoy the food on the table.

When I think about cooking Italian food, the first things that come to mind are memories of dining at Italian restaurants with my family. My parents used to take my little sister and me out for dinner on special occasions. We would savor the bread with its crispy and crunchy crust and its soft inside. I loved dipping it into the mixture of olive oil and garlic, but my sister always joked that it gave me bad breath! For my dinner I could never decide between pizza and pasta, so my sister and I would always each choose one and share. Dessert was always something chocolate topped with raspberries. The smells were irresistibly tempting, and the food lived up to the anticipation. I loved eating Italian food.

Being a California girl, I grew up eating Mexican food on a regular basis. My friends and I never went to diners; we always had a burrito place that we hung out at. My favorite was on Twenty-Fourth Street in San Francisco's Noe Valley area. It is called Casa Mexicana and is totally a hole-in-the-wall. You would walk in the front door and immediately get shuffled through a very organized line where you would need to point to the ingredients you wanted inside your burrito. They always used the freshest ingredients. I loved the combination of the warm pinto beans, rice, and grilled chicken meshing with the cold cheese, lettuce, salsa, sour cream, and guacamole when they wrapped it all up in a huge flour tortilla. It was absolutely the most satisfying meal.

My experience with Asian food goes all the way back to my mom having undiagnosed Celiac Disease while she was pregnant. One of the major complications of undiagnosed Celiac Disease is a condition called intrauterine growth retardation. This essentially means that a woman's placenta dies at about six or seven months, which can cause a number of problems for the baby. Worst-case scenario is a stillborn child. Best-case scenario is a very premature child, which is exactly what I was. My due date was June 1, 1983, but I popped out on April 12, screaming for food! I was attached to all sorts of tubes for weeks, and when I was finally sent home, I needed a full-time nurse to watch over me. Thus Thelma Rodin-DeSilva entered my life. Thelma had just come to the United States from the Philippines and was not only a skilled nurse, but also an amazing cook. She taught my mom everything about making Asian food, from finding the best ingredients at Asian markets to incorporating the intense flavors into our family's diet. I grew up eating chicken adobo, pineapple fried rice, spring rolls, cashew chicken, and even sushi. Yummy! I loved Asian food.

My background in eating delicious food was something that I prided myself on and enjoyed sharing. Whenever I went to restaurants with friends, I loved being the one who knew all about the food. But when I was diagnosed with Celiac Disease, I truly believed that my culinary life as I had known it had come to an end. Italian food is almost entirely made from wheat flour. Flour tortillas are a staple of Mexican cooking. Soy sauce is in almost every Asian dish, and it is impossible to find wonton or egg roll wrappers that are made without wheat.

Perfecting my recipes took years of work and experimentation with various gluten-free flours and grains, but all of it was deliciously worthwhile. Today I cook food that tastes exquisite to everyone whether or not they are on a special diet. Eating this food makes me feel normal, but the best feeling is when my friends and family eat the same meals as I do and love them, too.

As I became more skilled in the kitchen, I began working with the National Foundation for Celiac Awareness on projects to educate doctors and chefs about Celiac Disease. During this time, I met three incredibly special individuals: Chef Edgar Steele of Café Atlantico; Chef Katie Chin of Thai Kitchen, who is the author of *Everyday Chinese Cooking*, and Chef Keith Brunell of Maggiano's Little Italy. Each of them has embraced the idea of gluten-free cooking and has dedicated time to helping people with Celiac Disease learn that they can again enjoy the food they eat at restaurants.

Thanks to these wonderful chefs and inspiration from my grandmother's recipe box, I have completely changed my life. I am finally healthy and enjoy the food I eat. I can make it though an entire meal without running to the bathroom and confidently attend social functions without being fearful of embarrassing gas!

The gluten-free diet has restored my health and helped me live an incredible life. I hope my passion for food and my desire for good health will inspire you to reclaim yours as well.

In my first book, *Beyond Rice Cakes: A Young Person's Guide to Cooking, Eating & Living Gluten-Free*, I helped people diagnosed with Celiac Disease learn to overcome the challenges of beginning a gluten-free lifestyle by teaching them the basics of cooking easy-to-make recipes. *The Gloriously Gluten-Free Cookbook: Spicing Up Life with Italian, Asian, and Mexican Recipes* takes gluten-free cuisine to the next level—beyond the perimeters of the grocery store—and will teach you to cook Italian, Asian, and Mexican food that tastes like it came from a five-star restaurant. Your mouth will water and you'll count down the minutes until the food is ready . . . just like you were sitting at a table in a restaurant.

Every cuisine has its signature dishes, and in every case, they can be altered for a gluten-free diet. You can substitute a variety of gluten-free flours to make delicious Italian meals like pizza and calzones. Corn tortillas work just as well as flour tortillas in Mexican food. And, there are a variety of gluten-free soy sauces and rice noodles available to make delightful Asian food! Some substitutions take work, but I'm confident you'll find that the gluten-free versions in this book will taste just as good, if not better, than the originals.

Let's get started!

Living with CELIAC DISEASE

Living with Celiac Disease is a lifelong commitment that requires constant dedication and appreciation for both the disease itself and the food you put into your mouth every day. In order to properly manage the gluten-free lifestyle, it's important to learn a little about the nuts and bolts of Celiac Disease and how it actually affects your body.

What Is Celiac Disease?

Do you pass gas more obviously and frequently than other people? Need to run to the bathroom at all of the most inconvenient times? Experience severe migraine headaches, achiness, extreme fatigue, or an itchy skin rash on your elbows and knees? If so, it may be Celiac Disease causing these embarrassing problems.

Celiac Disease is an autoimmune digestive disorder that is triggered by eating the gluten protein, which is found in all forms of wheat, rye, and barley.

When a healthy person eats food, it travels to the small intestines, where it is absorbed into cells and broken down. Once the food particles are processed in the small intestine's cells, the cells release nutrients into the bloodstream where they are absorbed and used by the body to function.

If you have Celiac Disease, this whole process becomes disrupted when you eat gluten. Between the cells that are supposed to process food particles, we all have what are known as "tight junctions," which actually function like gates that can open and close. When a person with Celiac Disease eats gluten, the food travels into the small intestines, but accidentally slips past the cells through the gates. Most doctors call this "leaky gut" syndrome because the gut is essentially leaking out the gluten protein before it has a chance to be processed and digested through the cells.

The leaking of the gluten protein is essentially toxic for a person with Celiac Disease and causes damage to the villi in the small intestines, which makes it nearly impossible for the body to absorb nutrients into the bloodstream. If it isn't corrected quickly, it can lead to malnourishment and a host of other problems, including cancer, osteoporosis, infertility, diabetes, and thyroid disease.

Who Gets Celiac Disease?

More than one in every one hundred Americans have Celiac Disease, equivalent to about one percent of the U.S. population. However, because the disease is so difficult to diagnose, ninety-five percent of people with Celiac Disease remain undiagnosed or misdiagnosed. Translated into real numbers, this means that up to three million Americans have Celiac Disease, and only about 150,000 know they have the condition. The good news is that the latest research expects up to fifty percent of those in the U.S. with the undiagnosed disease to be diagnosed by 2018.

Symptoms of Celiac Disease

According to the National Institutes of Health, Celiac Disease is a common autoimmune digestive disease with a wide variety of symptoms that can manifest in dramatically different ways depending on the patient. One person might have stomachaches, while another might have an itchy skin rash, vitamin deficiencies, or headaches. With hundreds of symptoms linked to the disease, doctors often have difficulty diagnosing it and in many cases misdiagnose patients with other conditions. The most common misdiagnosis is Irritable Bowel Syndrome (IBS).

The most common symptoms of Celiac Disease are:

Abdominal pain

Anemia

Attention deficit disorder (ADD)

Attention-deficit/hyperactivity disorder (ADHD)

Bloating

Bone and joint pain

Constipation

Delayed growth in children

Depression

Dermatitis herpetiformis (itchy skin rash)

Diarrhea

Enamel defects on teeth

Fatigue

Fatty stools that float

Fractures or thin bones

Gas

Infertility or pregnancy complications

Migraine headaches

Nausea

Numbness in legs

Osteoporosis or osteopenia

Pale sores in mouth (canker sores)

Vitamin deficiencies

Although the list of symptoms is lengthy, some patients experience no symptoms at any time in their lives. However, if you are one of these patients and are diagnosed with Celiac Disease, it is imperative that you stick to the gluten-free diet to prevent long-term complications. Just because you don't feel a reaction doesn't mean your body isn't having one.

Related Diseases

A number of conditions are related to Celiac Disease and put patients in a high-risk group for also having Celiac Disease. These diseases include:

Dermatitis herpetiformis

Down syndrome

Intestinal cancer

Juvenile idiopathic arthritis

Peripheral neuropathy

Sjögren's syndrome

Thyroid disease

Turner syndrome

Type 1 diabetes

Williams syndrome

Diagnosis of
CELIAC DISEASE

Gaining an accurate Celiac diagnosis can be difficult in many cases, largely because there are so many symptoms that could suggest other diseases. For example, a digestive disease is probably not the first diagnosis a dermatologist will think of when a patient presents with a skin rash. And it's highly unlikely a neurologist will think of Celiac Disease first when a patient comes in complaining about recurring headaches. To determine if a patient has Celiac Disease, a doctor can order several different tests, including an antibody blood test, a genetic test, or a small-intestine biopsy. The following descriptions are verified by physicians at the Georgetown University Hospital Department of Gastroenterology.

Antibody Celiac Test

The antibody test for Celiac Disease is a blood test that measures anti-endomysium and anti-tissue transglutaminase. The antibody test determines whether or not a patient's body is creating a negative response to the gluten protein. If a person has Celiac Disease, he or she will have higher-than-normal antibody levels.

The antibody test is made up of a panel consisting of anti-tissue transglutaminase (IgA-tTG), total serum IgA, and endomysium antibody (IgA-EMA). To take the test, a patient must be eating a normal diet containing gluten. Most doctors will recommend eating about four servings per day for six weeks before having the antibody test, but it's important to discuss this with your personal physician before having the test.

A positive blood test is only the first step toward gaining an accurate diagnosis. After receiving a positive blood test, a patient will need a small-intestine biopsy to verify the Celiac diagnosis.

Genetic Testing

The genetic test for Celiac Disease is used for two very important reasons. The first is to determine the presence of the HLA-DQ2 and HLA-DQ8 genes. These are the genes directly linked to Celiac Disease and help a doctor determine if you are at risk for developing the disease. If these genes are not present, it is nearly impossible to develop Celiac Disease and no further testing is necessary. If the genes are present, additional testing such as the antibody test or endoscopy are required. This is a great way to rule out the disease among family members.

The second reason for the genetic test, and its most common use, is to determine a possible diagnosis in patients who are already living on a gluten-free diet, perhaps because a family member has

already been diagnosed with Celiac and the household is already gluten-free. Having the HLA-DQ2 and HLA-DQ8 genes does not definitely mean a person has Celiac Disease. In fact, about thirty percent of the U.S. population carries these genes, but only one percent will actually develop Celiac Disease. A positive genetic test will put you in a high-risk group for Celiac that requires further testing.

In the past, genetic testing for Celiac Disease was conducted by collecting a blood sample. These tests are incredibly expensive, especially when they don't actually provide a positive or negative diagnosis for the condition. However, Prometheus Labs (prometheuslabs.com) has developed a new at-home, saliva-based genetic test that will determine the presence of the genes linked to Celiac Disease without the need for a blood test.

The MyCeliacID test is approved by the Food and Drug Administration and is incredibly simple to use. The patient orders the test kit online, collects a saliva sample in the included test tube, and returns the sample to Prometheus Labs in a prepaid box that comes with the kit. Within seven days, Prometheus will send the confidential results. A negative test result means the genes are not present, and a positive test signifies you are a carrier for the Celiac genes and should seek further medical attention.

You can visit https://myceliacid.com for more information.

Small-Intestine Biopsy

If a patient receives either a positive antibody blood test or genetic test, it is almost always recommended that he or she receive a small-bowel biopsy to determine if there is damage to the villi. The villi are small fingerlike protrusions in the small intestines that are responsible for absorbing nutrients from food. When they are damaged it becomes almost impossible to absorb proper nutrients, which can lead to many long-term complications. The biopsy is done under anesthesia and involves the doctor using an endoscope, which is a long, thin tube threaded through the mouth and stomach to view the small intestines. The biopsy is the "gold standard" of diagnosis and the only definite way to determine if someone has Celiac Disease. However, there is hope on the horizon for a simpler way to diagnose the condition. Diagnostic companies are hard at work to develop blood tests that are as specific and reliable as the endoscopy. Several are FDA approved and are being evaluated to replace the biopsy.

Finger-Prick Test

The Biocard Celiac Test kit is an at-home test that measures IgA antibodies (anti-tTG) from a fingertip blood sample. It works by pricking your finger, mixing the blood with a buffer, and applying the mixture to a test cartridge. The test can be administered from home, and you'll get results in just ten minutes. If the test is positive for Celiac Disease, the makers of the test recommend consulting with a doctor to confirm the diagnosis with an intestinal biopsy.

According to the marketers at 2G Pharma Inc., the test is as accurate as a tissue transglutaminase (tTG) laboratory test that your doctor would request and uses the same technology to detect specific IgA antibodies that react with tissue transglutaminase, a well-known indicator of Celiac Disease. The test has been approved by Health Canada and meets all the European requirements for a home test.

A study published in the *British Medical Journal* found that a simple rapid antibody test—such as the finger-prick test— allowed nurses working in primary care medical offices to detect Celiac Disease in patients who were not diagnosed during routine clinical care. The study evaluated 2,690 children around six years old and 120 nurses. Out of 31 newly diagnosed Celiac patients, the rapid test accurately detected Celiac Disease in 30 patients. The test will soon be available to everyone in the United States through his or her doctor or by ordering the test kit online.

The Biocard Celiac Test is a landmark development for the Celiac community. For the first time patients will have the ability to find out immediately if they have the autoimmune disorder. It will also allow for simple mass screening, especially among family members of those already diagnosed.

Treatment:
LIVING ON A GLUTEN-FREE Diet

There is only one known treatment for Celiac Disease and it's simple: a lifelong gluten-free diet, eliminating all forms of wheat, rye, and barley. Although several pharmaceutical companies are working to develop a drug therapy, there are currently no medications or surgeries that can cure Celiac Disease.

Sticking to a strict gluten-free diet is vitally important for people with Celiac Disease. Eating any amount of gluten, no matter how small it is, can cause damage to the small intestines and prevent absorption of nutrients from food into the bloodstream.

Cheating on the diet is not an option and can lead to long-term complications, so resist temptation to cheat!

Several researchers are working tirelessly to develop medications to assist with the digestion of gluten, but to date, the most promising therapies will allow a patient to consume less than 2.5 grams of gluten per day. This is about a quarter of a slice of bread.

What Happens if You Eat Gluten?

Gluten is considered toxic to people with Celiac Disease. Although Celiacs will not experience anaphylactic shock if they eat gluten, they will have symptoms, such as diarrhea, abdominal pain, skin rashes, or headaches, among others. Eating gluten can also cause long-term damage to the small intestines that can lead to cancer, malnourishment, and other autoimmune conditions. There is no medical treatment to prevent, stop, or reduce the severity of the reaction once gluten has been ingested.

The good news? Patients who strictly follow the gluten-free diet can begin to experience relief of symptoms in as little as one week, although it typically takes up to six months for the small intestines to heal in children and up to two years to heal in adults.

How to Live with Celiac Disease

Eliminating popular gluten-containing foods such as pizza, pasta, cake, and cookies from the diet can seem overwhelming when you're first diagnosed. Believe me, I know! As a college kid when I learned I had Celiac Disease, it seemed like my world had come to an end when I couldn't order pizza delivery anymore. But let me assure you that with just a little extra effort and creativity in the kitchen, people with the disease can eat the delicious food that everyone loves.

12 STEPS TO LIVING A HEALTHY GLUTEN-FREE LIFE

The following are steps that you can follow to lead a healthy and worthwhile life after your Celiac diagnosis. It may seem slightly overwhelming at first, but don't worry! By the time you finish reading this book, you'll be well equipped to spend the rest of your life loving the food you eat and feeling healthy with every bite.

1. ACCEPT YOUR DIAGNOSIS AND STAY POSITIVE

The first step toward managing a successful gluten-free lifestyle is accepting that you need to be on the diet for your health. No one likes to be diagnosed with a disease, but if you had to have one, Celiac is one of the best! By simply changing your diet, you are on the road to a life filled with healthiness. Having a positive outlook will make managing the new way you eat so much easier. Just remember to have an open mind. Use the recipes in this book to prove to yourself and your family that gluten-free food is delicious!

2. SEEK PROFESSIONAL GUIDANCE FROM A DIETITIAN

Upon giving you a Celiac diagnosis, your doctor should refer you to a skilled dietitian. Dietitians can help you learn the basics of a gluten-free diet and make suggestions for managing it in a way that doesn't seem invasive and keeps you healthy. They can teach you about reading food labels and where to find the best products in your area. You can also download a Gluten-Free Survival Guide from the National Foundation for Celiac Awareness at www.celiaccentral.org.

3. LEARN WHICH FOODS CONTAIN GLUTEN AND AVOID THEM

Gluten is a protein found in all forms of wheat, barley, and rye. This means it is probably found in most of the breads, cookies, cakes, cereals, pastas, and other carbs you typically buy at the grocery store. You will need to learn all the unsafe ingredients to watch out for, as well as hidden sources of gluten.

Here is a list of things that contain the gluten protein:

Barley	Farro	Semolina
Bulgur	Graham	Spelt
Couscous	Kamut	Triticale
Durum	Malt flavoring	Wheat
Einkorn	Matzo	Wheat flour
Emmer	Mir	Wheat germ
Farina	Rye	Wheat starch

A SPECIAL CAUTION: **OATS**

Oats in their natural form do not contain gluten. However, most mills that produce oat products also process wheat. This means that there is a good chance the oats are contaminated. The good news is that there are now several manufacturers producing clean, safe oats for people with Celiac Disease. Bob's Red Mill, for example, has a dedicated mill for oats and certifies on their packaging that their oats are safe for those on a gluten-free diet.

4. LEARN WHICH FOODS ARE SAFE AND HOW TO USE THEM

There are tons of naturally gluten-free products available on the market, many of which produce better-tasting food than their gluten-containing counterparts. They are naturally grown products that can be seasoned and cooked into delicious, healthy, and safe meals. You can buy them at grocery stores, specialty markets, and ethnic markets and from food wholesale providers. Throughout this book, you'll learn how to use them to their fullest potential and discover some delicious new flavors.

Here is a basic list of gluten-free grains and flours:

Almond meal	Corn flour	Roasted kasha
Amaranth	Cornmeal	Sorghum flour
Arborio rice	Cornstarch	Soy
Arrowroot	Guar gum	Tapioca flour
Bean flours	Jasmine rice	Tapioca starch
Brown rice	Lentils	Teff
Brown rice flour	Potato flour	White rice
Buckwheat	Potato starch	White rice flour
Coconut flour	Quinoa	Xanthan gum

There are also many other naturally gluten-free products you'll always find at your local grocery store. They include:

Beef	Milk
Cheese	Nuts
Coffee	Pork
Eggs	Poultry
Fresh seafood	Sour cream/yogurt
Fruits	Vegetables

5. LEARN HOW TO READ FOOD LABELS

Gluten is added to foods that you might not suspect. You must learn to read food labels carefully to ensure that what you buy is safe. This particularly applies to canned and packaged foods. Recent food labeling laws mandate that manufacturers list the eight most common allergens on food labels. The law includes wheat, but does not include gluten, so be sure to always double-check for rye and barley.

6. RESEARCH GLUTEN-FREE VENDORS AND SPECIALTY PRODUCTS

The gluten-free marketplace is rapidly expanding. More and more people are being diagnosed with Celiac Disease every day and the market is responding in turn with more and better-tasting gluten-free options. Today there are pizza crusts, pastas, cookies, and cakes—all tasting close to normal! These products are available in mainstream grocery stores such as Giant Foods, Stop & Shop, Whole Foods, Wegmans, Safeway, Publix, and even Walmart. If your store doesn't have these on the shelves, speak to someone in customer service; in most cases, they can order what you need.

7. BUY GLUTEN-FREE COOKBOOKS, READ BLOGS AND LEARN TO COOK

There are hundreds of cookbooks that can teach you to cook delicious gluten-free recipes. Head down to your local bookstore or search online, and start browsing through the specialty-diets-cookbook section. You'll find books addressing basic cooking techniques, baking, and even cooking for kids. Start exploring simple recipes that you can make for yourself and your family that make use of naturally gluten-free ingredients.

I'm usually very cautious about recommending the use of the Internet for finding health information, but the World Wide Web provides a fantastic platform for learning about gluten-free food. There are tons of bloggers dedicated just to helping people learn about gluten-free cooking and dining out at restaurants, so head online and Google "gluten-free food blogs." You'll find everything from classy gluten-free cooking to simple recipes, vegetarian options, dairy-free cooking, and any other combination of recipes you can think of. Some blogs are even dedicated to writing restaurant reviews to help you find the best gluten-free places to eat around the world. Be sure to check out my Celiac Princess blog at www.celiacprincess.com. I post new gluten-free recipes several times a week, so you'll never be without a gluten-free dinner idea.

Here are some of my other favorite bloggers:

Celiac Chicks • www.celiacchicks.com

Elana's Pantry • www.elanaspantry.com

Gluten-Free Goddess • www.glutenfreegoddess.blogspot.com

Gluten-Free Girl • www.glutenfreegirl.com

Sugar & Spice: My Gluten-Free Life • www.alifeofsugarandspice.com

Triumph Dining • blog.triumphdining.com

8. PREVENT CROSS-CONTAMINATION AT HOME

Learning to prevent cross-contamination is absolutely necessary for keeping to a perfect gluten-free diet. This means learning to keep everything that's gluten-free away from things containing gluten. This also applies to cooking surfaces, utensils, condiments, frying oil, boiling water, and food preparation areas. But don't worry if the rest of your family is not on a gluten-free diet. A kitchen does not need to be one hundred percent gluten-free as long as you have devised a way to prevent contamination of gluten-free food.

Here are some ideas for keeping your kitchen safe:

Boiling water. You must use clean water when cooking food such as gluten-free pasta, rice, vegetables, or quinoa. This is also true for colanders. Noodles can stick between the cracks, so scrub well!

Condiments. Any condiment that requires you to dip a utensil into it should not be used for both gluten-free and gluten-containing food. One way to ensure your safety is to have two containers of condiments like cream cheese. Or, just be very careful not to double dip. For condiments such as mayonnaise, ketchup, and mustard, squeeze bottles are a good way to prevent contamination.

Cutting boards. Unless you plan to thoroughly wash a cutting board before use with gluten-free foods, it is helpful to have a designated gluten-free cutting board. Try color coding or labeling the second board so everyone in your household knows to use only gluten-free food on that board. Be consistent and don't get lazy. If the gluten-free board is dirty, spend the extra minute to wash it instead of using a non-gluten-free board. Even the slightest bit of contamination can make you sick.

Frying. Do not fry gluten-free foods in the same oil you use to fry foods that contains gluten. Gluten particles come off in the oil and will contaminate your gluten-free food. Even if the oil looks clean, there is still a chance of contamination, so to be safe; always use clean oil. Also, be sure to always clean frying pans thoroughly between uses.

Pots and pans. Be scrupulous about using clean pots or pans to cook gluten-free food. Clean them before each use, just as you'd do to prevent food poisoning!

Toaster ovens. Some families choose to have separate toaster ovens—one for gluten-free food and a second one for everything else. This is an easy way to prevent contamination. [But it does take up a lot of counter space. Simply cleaning out the toaster oven after use will get rid of crumbs and allow everyone to use the same toaster. Be sure to clean both inside the toaster oven and the racks.]

Utensils. When you're cooking, don't use the utensils for gluten-free food that you have already used for gluten-containing food. For example, don't use the same spoon to stir gluten-free pasta that you have just used for regular pasta. Either wash your utensils thoroughly after each use or have a set that you designate gluten-free.

9. EDUCATE YOUR FAMILY

Your family must play a role in your gluten-free diet. Everyone needs to understand what the diet entails and how to prevent cross-contamination. Simply remind your family not to share utensils, pots and pans, toaster ovens, and other cookware without thoroughly cleaning them. For example, teach your family not to double dip in condiments and to always clean up after working with gluten-containing foods in the kitchen.

Also, be sure to teach your family that gluten-free food is delicious! And they will be shocked at how many recipes you can make that are naturally gluten-free. Having a supportive family is imperative to managing Celiac Disease. Help your family understand early on that a gluten-free diet is a major lifestyle change that they need to help with. A mistake on their part could cause you extreme discomfort and long-term medical complications.

10. FIND SUPPORT GROUP

Every state in the United States has at least one, if not several, Celiac support groups. They are run by one of three organizations: the Celiac Sprue Association, the Celiac Disease Foundation, or the Gluten Intolerance Group (page 217, 218). Look up your local chapter and attend a meeting. You will meet people from your community and learn which restaurants are gluten free friendly. Vendors send product samples to most meetings, so this is a great opportunity to taste the best new gluten-free products. Or, join a Celiac Disease Meet-Up group. Many of these are dining groups that try out all of the best restaurants in their area. Check them out at www.meetup.com

11. SCHEDULE ANNUAL FOLLOW-UP APPOINTMENTS WITH YOUR DOCTOR

To make sure the gluten-free diet is in fact helping your intestines heal, schedule annual exams with your doctor. You will need to take the Celiac antibody test. If your blood test comes back normal, it will confirm that the diet is working. However, it is important to remember that a normal blood test does *not* mean that your Celiac has gone away. Celiac Disease is not curable, and you will have it for the rest of your life. You must always maintain a gluten-free diet.

It is also important to have your family members tested for Celiac. It is a genetic disease, meaning it is passed on through families. Even if your family members have no apparent symptoms, it is still crucial to have them tested. An early diagnosis can prevent devastating complications later in life.

12. START COOKING . . . AND USING THIS COOKBOOK!

Now that you've made it to step twelve, you're ready to head into the kitchen and start cooking. You'll find three sections of delicious recipes ahead: Italian, Asian, and Mexican. Each section starts with a note from a prestigious chef. After you learn all about the cuisines you'll find my list of recommendations for products to always keep on hand.

And then, of course, there are the recipes! Each top chef has contributed ten recipes. The rest are favorites from my own kitchen that I hope will convince you that gluten-free food is delicious and amazing.

Types of
GLUTEN-FREE FLOURS AND GRAINS

Thank you to Bob's Red Mill (www.bobsredmill.com) for help with preparing this list. The company manufactures flours and grains in a dedicated mill to ensure the integrity of its gluten-free production process.

Almond flour is made from raw blanched whole almonds that have been ground into a fine powder. Use almond meal in cakes, cookies, sweet breads, and a host of other desserts. You will get a fantastic rich flavor.

Amaranth flour developed in South America. It is typically used to replace twenty-five percent of the flour in a recipe and works well when combined with other flours such as tapioca and potato flours.

Amaranth grain is high in protein and fiber. It has a nutty flavor and can be combined with other gluten-free grains in breads, pastas, pancakes, and other recipes.

Brown rice flour is finely ground brown rice grains. Combine it with other flours to make gluten-free baked goods.

Coconut flour is a delicious, healthy alternative to gluten-containing flours. It is very high in fiber and very low in carbohydrates. It gives baked goods a rich texture and adds a natural sweetness. You'll need only about half the sugar you'd normally use when you bake with coconut flour.

Corn flour is fantastic for Latin-American cooking. It is used to make tamales, empanadas, and corn tortillas.

Cornstarch is a wonderful thickener for sauces. It works best when first dissolved in cold water. That prevents lumps from forming in a sauce.

Guar gum is typically used as a thickening agent. Use just a small amount in your recipes.

Potato starch is used as a thickener for sauces and soups. It can be cooked at higher temperatures than cornstarch.

Quinoa flour is rich in protein, calcium, and iron. You can use it in cookies, cakes, and even breads. It is healthier than white or brown rice flour.

Quinoa grain is the most "nutritious grain available." High in protein and rich in amino acids, it can be used as a healthy alternative to rice.

Roasted kasha is a fantastic grain that is typically used in hot cereals. It is widely available and is a great gluten-free choice.

Sorghum flour is packed with nutrition and adds a fantastic flavor to gluten-free baking. It is also great for making bread and potsticker dough.

Soy flour is made from soybeans ground into a fine powder. It is high in fiber and protein and gives baked goods a fantastic lightness.

Tapioca flour is derived from cassava root. It is slightly sweet and very starchy. Reduce the amount of sugar in your recipes slightly and combine the tapioca flour with other gluten-free options such as quinoa flour and brown rice flour.

White rice flour is finely stone-ground grains of white rice. Use it in combination with other flours for making gluten-free breads.

Xanthan gum is an incredible ingredient used to provide volume and thickness to gluten-free baked goods such as breads. It is a great all-purpose thickener, but be careful to use no more than 1/3 teaspoon per cup of flour in baking. A little bit goes a long way!

Italian
GLUTEN-FREE
COOKING

Chef's Note

FROM EXECUTIVE CHEF
Keith Brunell
of Maggiano's Little Italy

In Little Italy, meals aren't made, they're nurtured.
—MARCO, HEAD MAITRE D' AT MAGGIANO'S

At Maggiano's, we believe everyone can enjoy Italian food, especially those with special dietary needs, such as Celiac Disease or food allergies. No one should have to sacrifice the flavors they love—what's the fun in that? We want to help you feed all the guests around your table with great recipes such as baked ziti and garlic shrimp linguine with a rich wine sauce.

Cooking Italian food is simple. Use the freshest ingredients you can find and use basic cooking techniques and seasonings to bring out the natural flavors of the food. Garlic, thyme, rosemary, sage, oregano, parsley, marjoram, bay leaves, and basil are some of the most common herbs used in Italian cooking.

If you travel to Italy to experience the cuisine firsthand, you'll find the ingredients and dishes prepared vary greatly by region. Even cooking times and seasonings are regionally influenced. Beef, veal, and pork dishes are popular in the Northern region. Tomato-based dishes and grilled meats are traditional in Central Italy, as are leafy vegetables that can withstand the extreme climate. Southern Italy is well known for its use of vegetables and desserts. And, of course, fish and seafood dishes are coveted in the coastal regions. In all areas of Italy, wine and cheese are staples of most meals, as is espresso.

In the United States we put a spin on all of the fresh ingredients and cooking techniques used in Italy to create Italian American cuisine. This is our specialty at Maggiano's, and the good news is that most of these dishes are naturally gluten-free. Grilled calamari, risottos, and eggplant rollatini are just a few examples.

Pizza and pasta are a little bit more difficult for those on a gluten-free diet. But with some simple substitutions, you can enjoy these dishes too. For example, try brown rice or corn pasta in place of wheat pasta. Or, as you'll see in the recipes ahead, try using a variety of gluten-free flours to make a pizza crust. Or, forgo the flour altogether and use eggplant or large mushrooms as the crust. As long as you stick to the same herbs and spices, you'll have a delicious pizza or pasta the gluten-free way.

Personally, I think you're really going to enjoy these recipes. As a chef, I have dealt with many different dietary needs and food allergies. At Maggiano's Little Italy, we don't see these as limitations. Instead, we work harder to develop new ways to make sure we can welcome everyone in our restaurants. These dishes will allow all of your guests to share and sample the same foods knowing that their needs are taken care of.

Sometimes it can be challenging to find ways to change recipes without affecting their authenticity, but it's well worth the effort. I remember a visit from one woman in particular; she came in to have lunch with a client, and she called ahead to tell us about her Celiac Disease. I went to their table to explain all of our gluten-free options and to assure her the food would be prepared separately from everyone else's and that we could make a gluten-free substitution in almost any dish.

She said she was thrilled to be able to choose from items on our regular menu. She and her friend shared the spinach salad. Then she ordered corn pasta with tomato sauce mixed with chicken and sun-dried tomatoes. I went back to their table at the end of the meal. The woman nearly cried, she was so happy to have that experience. I could tell she had faced difficulties at other restaurants. To thank her for visiting Maggiano's, we gave her a bag of our corn pasta to enjoy at home. For me, this is why I love being a part of Maggiano's. What kind of chef would I be if I couldn't cook for everyone?

As I reflect back on that moment, it makes me feel even more confident in empowering you, the home cook, to learn to prepare delicious gluten-free food at home. Just because you're on a gluten-free diet doesn't mean you can't eat wonderful food. If a large restaurant chain can adapt in an industrial kitchen, you can adjust your home kitchen to be just as good, if not better.

Each Italian dish in this book has all the flavors of Little Italy—fresh basil, quality meats, sauces made from scratch—combined with corn and rice pastas cooked to perfection. Nice thing is, you can make these recipes your own. Add a little more of this or none of that—whatever it takes to make sure every one is fully satisfied. My hope is that you'll take the lessons in this book and head to the kitchen. Grab a bunch of parsley and some tomatoes and start cooking. I think you'll be impressed with yourself.

Enjoy giving your family and guests the best of Little Italy in your home. Be sure to make plenty for everyone, and while you're at it, put a few extra chairs at the table. They won't stay empty for long. And when you have a moment, invite your family and friends to come visit us here at Maggiano's Little Italy. We understand there are a few options for guests with Celiac Disease—and we are happy to become the top choice for these guests, by accommodating their needs. It's part of our mission.

Come by soon!
We'd love to see you.

ITALIAN INGREDIENTS *to Keep in Your Kitchen*

To be prepared for cooking Italian dishes, you'll want to have all of the essential spices and specialty items on hand. Thanks to a surge in awareness of the gluten-free diet, most mainstream grocery stores now stock all of the food products you'll need for a tasty gluten-free Italian meal. Below you'll find my favorites. Most of these are available at my regular grocery store. If you can't find these items in your area, be sure to speak to the store manager. Most stores are happy to order specialty items if they know a customer is going to purchase them.

SPICES

I always purchase McCormick spices (www.mccormick .com). It's their company policy to always declare on the label if any one of twelve allergens is used in their products, including wheat. If there is no declaration on the package, the only ingredient in the container is the pure spice.

Garlic powder

Ground cinnamon

Onion powder

Oregano

Parsley flakes

Thyme

FLOURS AND GRAINS

I always purchase Bob's Red Mill brand flours and grains because the company certifies on their packaging that each item was produced in a facility that is free of any gluten-containing ingredients. For rice, I generally purchase Lundberg (www.lundberg.com) or Rice Select (www.riceselect .com) brands because both companies have information available about the gluten-free status of their products.

Arborio rice

Brown rice flour

Potato starch

Quinoa

Soy flour

Tapioca flour

White rice flour

Xanthan gum

GLUTEN-FREE PASTA

There are several varieties of gluten-free pasta available at mainstream grocery stores. My personal favorite brand is Tinkyáda brown rice pasta. It comes in every possible shape and tastes just like regular pasta. They certify on their packaging that the brown rice pasta is wheat-free and gluten-free. Here is a list of Tinkyáda pasta, as well as other brands and varieties that are available.

DE BOLES
WWW.DEBOLES.COM

Angel hair

Fettuccine

Lasagna noodles

Penne

Spaghetti

Spirals

GLUTANO

Animal shapes

Spaghetti

Spirals

HEARTLAND'S FINEST

Elbows

Lasagna noodles

Linguine

Rotini

Spaghetti

Ziti

ORGRAN
WWW.ORGRAN.COM

Macaroni

Penne

Shells

Spirals

TINKYÁDA
WWW.TINKYADA.COM

Elbows

Fettuccine

Fusilli

Lasagna noodles

Penne

Shells

Spaghetti

Spirals

PREMADE PIZZA CRUSTS

The recipe for pizza crust in this book (page 78) is amazing, but if you don't have time to make your own, there are a few premade crusts that will work as a substitute. Whole Foods Gluten-Free Bakehouse (www.wholefoodsmarket.com) makes the best-tasting crust, but others are available for order through www.glutenfreemall.com. One is from Dad's gluten-free pizza crust (www.glutenfreepizza.com) and another from the Brazilian Cheese Bread Company (www.braziliancheesebreadco.com). You can also purchase mixes that only require you to add a few ingredients. Bob's Red Mill (www.bobsredmill.com) and Pamela's Products (www.pamelasproducts.com) both have wonderful pizza crust mixes that taste delicious!

OTHER INGREDIENTS

There are so many wonderful ingredients used in Italian cooking. Here are a few of the ingredients most frequently used throughout the book that you may want to keep on hand.

Arugula

Baking powder

Baking soda

Cheeses (a variety, but staples including

Parmesan and mozzarella cheese)

Cornstarch

Dry milk powder

Fresh basil

Fresh parsley

Garlic

Olive oil

Onions

Tomatoes

Tomato paste

Tomato sauce

SAUCES

A sauce completes a dish and brings out the flavors of every component. The sauces that follow are ten of my favorites from Italian cuisine. Each is filled with intense flavors and can be served with any type of pasta or protein. To make any sauce be vegetarian, substitute vegetable stock for chicken stock. For dairy-free sauces, replace heavy cream with plain soy milk.

Marinara Sauce

Marinara is one of the easiest sauces to make and is used in a variety of Italian dishes such as pastas, pizzas, calzones, and chicken or eggplant Parmesan. This recipe is my simple version, but you can spice it up with chili flakes and red or green bell peppers for a more intense flavor.

MAKES
1 QUART

● DAIRY-FREE

■ VEGETARIAN

¼ cup olive oil

2 yellow onions, diced

3 tablespoons minced garlic

1 tablespoon dried oregano

6 fresh basil leaves, chopped

One 28-ounce can diced
   tomatoes, undrained

1 tablespoon sugar

2 teaspoons salt

1 teaspoon freshly ground
   black pepper

1. In a large saucepan, heat the oil over medium-high heat. Add the onions, garlic, and oregano and cook, stirring, until softened, 5 to 7 minutes. Add the basil and cook, stirring, until wilted, about 1 minute more.

2. Add the diced tomatoes, including the liquid in the can, and sugar. Remove from the heat and, using an immersion blender, blend until smooth. (You may also transfer the contents of the pan to a traditional blender to do this, but be careful because the sauce will be hot.) Return the sauce to the heat, bring to a boil, then reduce the heat, cover, and simmer for 10 minutes. Remove from the heat, add the salt and pepper, and stir well.

3. Serve the sauce immediately over gluten-free pasta or, once cooled, store in an airtight container. The sauce will keep in the refrigerator for up to 5 days. You can freeze the sauce for up to 3 months.

Meat Sauce

This is essentially a heartier version of a marinara sauce. Lean ground beef is used here but you can use ground turkey or chicken if you're not a red meat lover.

MAKES
2 QUARTS

● DAIRY-FREE

¼ cup olive oil

1 yellow onion, diced

1 pound lean ground beef

1 tablespoon dried oregano

1 teaspoon chili flakes

1 recipe Marinara Sauce (page 31), or one 32-ounce can tomato sauce

Salt and freshly ground black pepper

1. In a large saucepan, heat the oil over medium-high heat. Add the onions, and cook, stirring, until lightly browned, 4 to 5 minutes. Add the beef and cook, stirring to break it up into small pieces, until well browned and no pink spots remain, 10 to 12 minutes. Remove from the heat and drain the excess fat from the pan. Return to medium heat, add the oregano and chili flakes, and simmer for 3 to 5 minutes. Stir in the Marinara Sauce, and simmer, stirring often, for 8 to 10 minutes more. Remove from the heat, add salt and pepper to taste, and stir well.

2. Serve the sauce immediately over gluten-free pasta or, once cooled, store in an airtight container. The sauce will keep in the refrigerator for up to 5 days. You can freeze the sauce for up to 3 months.

Pesto Sauce

The most important thing to remember when making a pesto sauce is to taste it often and create the blend of ingredients that you think tastes best. I like to use a combination of basil, arugula, and parsley, but you can use just basil. If you're going to use the sauce in pasta, pine nuts are a great idea. For pizza, a smoother pesto tends to work best.

MAKES
2 CUPS

▬ VEGETARIAN

½ pound fresh basil, rinsed and thoroughly dried, leaves removed and stems discarded

1 bunch arugula

½ bunch fresh parsley

¼ cup freshly grated Parmesan cheese

2 tablespoons extra-virgin olive oil

Salt and freshly ground black pepper

½ cup pine nuts (optional)

1. In a food processor, combine the basil, arugula, parsley, cheese, and 1 tablespoon of the oil and slowly puree, making sure everything is chopped, but not pureed into a liquid. If the mixture appears too thick, add the remaining 1 tablespoon of the oil. Add salt and pepper to taste. If using, add the pine nuts and blend until finely chopped and incorporated.

2. Serve the sauce immediately over gluten-free pasta or, when cooled, store in an airtight container. The sauce will keep in the refrigerator for up to 5 days.

White Wine and Garlic Sauce

This wonderful light sauce goes perfectly on pasta with grilled vegetables. The flavor is subtle and delicious. For a creamier version, add ½ cup of skim milk. If you have an allergy to potato starch, you can replace it with cornstarch.

MAKES
1 QUART

■ VEGETARIAN

3 tablespoons olive oil

1 cup diced yellow onion

2 tablespoons minced garlic

2 tablespoons potato starch

3 cups vegetable stock

2 cups white wine
(Chardonnay or Sauvignon
Blanc works best)

1 tablespoon butter

1 teaspoon salt

1 teaspoon freshly ground
black pepper

1. In a large saucepan, heat the oil over medium-high heat. Add the onions and garlic and cook, stirring often, until the onions become translucent, 5 to 7 minutes. Add in the potato starch and stir well until a thickened mixture forms, about 1 to 2 minutes. Mix in the stock and wine and cook, stirring often, until the sauce is reduced by about half, about 10 minutes. Add the butter, stir to combine as it melts, and simmer until the desired thickness is reached, about 5 minutes. Season with the salt and pepper.

2. Serve the sauce immediately over gluten-free pasta or, when cooled, store in an airtight container. The sauce will keep in the refrigerator for up to 5 days. You can freeze it for up to 3 months.

Cabernet–Garlic Sauce

I love the deep and complex flavor of this sauce, and the color is absolutely gorgeous. Try serving it over brown rice pasta and grilled eggplant. If you're allergic to potato starch, you can replace it with cornstarch.

MAKES 1 QUART

VEGETARIAN

3 tablespoons olive oil

1 cup diced yellow onion

1 tablespoon minced garlic

2 tablespoons potato starch

2 cups Cabernet Sauvignon wine

2 cups vegetable stock

1 cup heavy cream

1 tablespoon butter

1 teaspoon salt

1. In a large saucepan, heat the oil over medium-high heat, add the onions and garlic, and cook, stirring, until the onions become translucent, 5 to 7 minutes. Add in the potato starch and stir well until a thickened mixture forms, about 1 to 2 minutes. Stir in the wine and stock and cook until the sauce is reduced by about half, about 10 minutes. Add the cream and butter, stir to combine as it melts, and simmer until the desired thickness is reached, 5 to 7 minutes. Season with the salt.

2. Serve the sauce immediately over gluten-free pasta or, once cooled, store in an airtight container. The sauce will keep in the refrigerator for up to 5 days. You can freeze it for up to 3 months.

Alfredo Sauce

Everyone, especially kids, will love this cheesy sauce. Serve it over gluten-free pasta with steamed broccoli or use it to make a white pizza.

MAKES
1 QUART

▪ VEGETARIAN

4 cups heavy cream

2 tablespoons minced garlic

1 cup freshly grated Parmesan cheese

1 tablespoon butter

1 teaspoon salt

1 teaspoon freshly ground black pepper

1. In a large saucepan, heat the cream and garlic over medium-high heat and cook, stirring often, until the mixture begins to boil, 7 to 8 minutes. Remove from the heat and add the cheese and butter, blending until mixed thoroughly. Season with the salt and pepper.

2. Serve the sauce immediately over gluten-free pasta or, once cooled, store in an airtight container. The sauce will keep in the refrigerator for up to 5 days. You can freeze it for up to 3 months.

Rosemary-Beer Sauce

Gluten-free beer tastes just as wonderful as regular beer, and this sauce proves it! My grandma used to make this sauce with an amber beer; this is my interpretation using the new gluten-free Redbridge beer. You'll find the beer in most specialty grocery stores, and any liquor store can order it. If you're allergic to potato starch, you can replace it with cornstarch.

MAKES
1 QUART

● DAIRY-FREE
■ VEGETARIAN

3 tablespoons olive oil

1 tablespoon minced garlic

1 teaspoon chopped fresh rosemary, or ½ teaspoon crumbled dried rosemary

1 tablespoon potato starch

One 12-ounce bottle Redbridge gluten-free beer

1 cup vegetable stock

1 teaspoon salt

1 teaspoon freshly ground black pepper

1. In a large saucepan, heat the oil over medium-low heat. Add the garlic and rosemary and cook, stirring, until softened, 4 to 5 minutes. Add in the potato starch and stir well until a thickened mixture forms, about 1 to 2 minutes. Mix in the beer and stock and cook, stirring frequently, for about 10 minutes. Season with the salt and pepper.

2. Serve the sauce immediately over gluten-free pasta or, once cooled, store in an airtight container. The sauce will keep in the refrigerator for up to 5 days. You can freeze it for up to 3 months.

Cherry Tomato Sauce

Serve this simple and delicious sauce over gluten-free pasta or pour it over chicken before baking.

MAKES
1 QUART

● DAIRY-FREE
■ VEGETARIAN

2 tablespoons olive oil

2 tablespoons minced garlic

1 teaspoon chili flakes

6 cups cherry tomatoes, cut in half or chopped if large

Two 8-ounce cans tomato sauce

2 cups vegetable stock

⅓ cup chopped fresh basil leaves

1 teaspoon freshly grated lemon zest

1 teaspoon salt

1 teaspoon freshly ground black pepper

1. In a large saucepan, heat the oil over medium-low heat. Add the garlic and chili flakes and cook, stirring constantly, until the garlic is lightly browned, 4 to 5 minutes. Add the tomatoes and cook, stirring lightly, until the tomatoes are softened, about 3 minutes. Add the tomato sauce, stock, basil, and lemon zest and cook until the sauce comes to a simmer, about 10 minutes. Season with the salt and pepper.

2. Serve the sauce immediately over gluten-free pasta or, once cooled, store in an airtight container. The sauce will keep in the refrigerator for up to 5 days. You can freeze it for up to 3 months.

Creamy Parmesan Sauce

This is a lush, cheesy sauce that can be used over pasta or as an accompaniment to steamed vegetables. I love steaming broccoli and cauliflower and pouring the sauce over it. If you're allergic to potato starch, you can replace it with cornstarch.

MAKES
1 QUART

VEGETARIAN

6 tablespoons olive oil

½ cup diced yellow onion

2 tablespoons minced garlic

1 tablespoon potato starch

2 cups vegetable stock

2 cups white wine, such as Chardonnay

2 cups freshly grated Parmesan cheese

1 tablespoon Italian seasoning

1 teaspoon salt

1 teaspoon freshly ground black pepper

1. In a large saucepan, heat the oil over medium-high heat. Add the onions and garlic and cook, stirring, until the onions become translucent, 5 to 7 minutes. Add in the potato starch and stir well until a thickened mixture forms, about 1 to 2 minutes. Stir in the stock and wine and bring to a boil, then reduce the heat to medium, cover, and simmer for about 5 minutes. Gently stir in the cheese and Italian seasoning. Cook, stirring constantly, until the cheese is melted and blended into the sauce. Season with the salt and pepper.

2. Serve the sauce immediately over gluten-free pasta or, once cooled, store in an airtight container. The sauce will keep in the refrigerator for up to 5 days. You can freeze it for up to 3 months.

Vodka Sauce

Vodka sauce is a wonderful, simple, and flavorful sauce that goes well with most proteins. My favorite way to serve it is over turkey meatballs with pasta, but other suggestions include pasta with ground beef, lobster, or chicken.

MAKES
1 QUART

■ VEGETARIAN

¼ cup olive oil

1 tablespoon butter

1 cup finely diced yellow onion

2 garlic cloves, minced

2 cups heavy cream (can use half-and-half or light cream)

One 8-ounce can peeled tomatoes, chopped

One 8-ounce can tomato sauce

½ cup vodka

⅓ cup chopped fresh parsley

⅓ cup freshly grated Parmesan cheese

Salt and freshly ground black pepper

1. In a medium saucepan, heat the oil and butter over medium-high heat. Add the onions and garlic, and cook, stirring, until the onions become translucent, 5 to 7 minutes. Add in the cream, tomatoes, tomato sauce, vodka, and parsley. Bring sauce to simmer, stirring frequently, for 8 to 10 minutes. Stir in the cheese until blended. Add salt and pepper to taste.

2. Serve the sauce immediately over gluten-free pasta or, once cooled, store in an airtight container. The sauce will keep in the refrigerator for up to 5 days. You can freeze the sauce for up to 3 months.

STARTERS

Most Italian meals start with some sort of bread product that contains gluten. These are some of my favorite starters which I've converted to gluten-free form, and also a few that are naturally gluten-free. The first time I made the crab cakes and breadsticks, I almost cried tears of joy! They tasted . . . normal.

Artichoke-Parmesan Salad with Dijon Mustard Dressing

This recipe combines several of my favorite ingredients that I rarely use together, and I created it on a total whim. The night before I was moving out of my apartment to a new, bigger one with my awesome, food-loving fiancé, I was desperately looking for something to eat for dinner so that I didn't have to order takeout. I found three cans of artichokes that I hadn't wanted to pack, so I started going through my refrigerator to find things that would mesh well with them. This salad turned out to be delicious; it was simple to prepare, and made more than enough for lunch the next day! Be sure to use only plain artichokes. Many of the marinated varieties are not gluten-free.

MAKES
4 SERVINGS

■ VEGETARIAN

2 tablespoons olive oil

1 tablespoon fresh lemon juice

1 teaspoon Dijon mustard

1 garlic clove, mashed to a
  paste

½ teaspoon salt

Three 8-ounce cans artichoke
  hearts, drained and sliced

1 cup freshly grated Parmesan
  cheese

1 cup diced tomatoes

¼ cup finely chopped fresh
  parsley

1. In a medium bowl, whisk together the oil, lemon juice, mustard, garlic, and salt. Add the artichoke hearts, cheese, tomatoes, and parsley and, using a large spoon, gently toss all together. Chill before serving.

Crab Cakes

I love crab cakes, but sadly, most are made with breadcrumbs. This recipe produces cakes that taste just like my old restaurant favorites and uses no breadcrumbs at all. If you have an allergy to potato starch, you can replace it with cornstarch and achieve the same results. If time allows, make the tartar sauce in advance and refrigerate it until ready to serve.

MAKES 8
CRAB CAKES

1 pound fresh jumbo lump crabmeat

2 large eggs

¼ cup chopped celery

¼ cup chopped scallions

¼ cup mayonnaise

¼ cup potato starch

2 tablespoons chopped fresh parsley

1 teaspoon dry mustard

1 teaspoon fresh lemon juice

1 teaspoon Old Bay seasoning

1 teaspoon Worcestershire sauce

2 to 3 dashes hot sauce

½ teaspoon salt

½ teaspoon freshly ground black pepper

Oil or butter, for sautéeing

Tartar sauce, for serving

1. In a large bowl, stir together the crabmeat, eggs, celery, scallions, mayonnaise, potato starch, parsley, mustard, lemon juice, Old Bay seasoning, Worcestershire sauce, hot sauce, salt, and pepper, being sure to thoroughly incorporate all of the ingredients. Cover with plastic wrap and chill in the refrigerator for about 20 minutes.

2. Divide crab mixture into 8 equal portions of about ½ cup. Using your hands, form the portions into round cakes. In a skillet, heat the oil or butter over medium-high heat and gently set each crab cake in the pan, adding them in batches if necessary. Cook until lightly browned, 6 to 8 minutes per side. Serve immediately with tartar sauce.

Tartar Sauce

MAKES 1 CUP

VEGETARIAN

¼ cup sour cream

1 scallion, chopped finely

3 tablespoons mayonnaise

1 tablespoon fresh lemon juice

1 tablespoon chopped fresh parsley

1 tablespoon capers, chopped

½ teaspoon hot sauce (optional)

1. In a small bowl, combine all ingredients and mix well. Serve with crab cakes.

Sautéed Calamari

This recipe comes from the kitchen of Chef Keith Brunell of Maggiano's Little Italy. The first time I ate the gluten-free version of calamari at Maggiano's, I was the happiest girl! Usually when calamari is made without a breading, it tastes bland and boring. This version is full of flavor. Try it on its own, in a salad, or over a bed of rice.

MAKES
4 SERVINGS

1 tablespoon olive oil

1 pound calamari, cleaned and cut into -inch rings

1 tablespoon minced garlic

1 tablespoon white wine

2 tablespoons diced Roma tomatoes

1 tablespoon butter

1 tablespoon fresh lemon juice

1 teaspoon chili flakes

1 teaspoon salt

1 teaspoon freshly ground black pepper

1. In a large sauté pan, heat the oil over high heat until slightly smoking. Add the calamari and cook, stirring, until lightly browned, 1 to 2 minutes. Reduce the heat to medium-high, add the garlic, and cook, stirring, for 30 seconds. Add the wine and cook, stirring, 5 to 6 minutes more. Add the tomatoes, butter, lemon juice, and chili flakes and cook, stirring gently, until the tomatoes have softened and the butter is completely melted, 4 to 5 minutes. Season with the salt and pepper and serve.

● DAIRY-FREE OPTION

Eliminate the butter and add an additional tablespoon of olive oil.

Italian Breadsticks

Warm, soft breadsticks were one of the things I craved after I went on the gluten-free diet. This recipe makes delicious breadsticks that taste like they came straight out of the oven at a famous Italian restaurant. Try dipping them in olive oil or marinara sauce for an even bigger flavor. I like to sprinkle Parmesan cheese on top before baking, but you can add any spices you want. You can also use whole eggs in the recipe, but using just the egg whites lightens the texture.

MAKES 12
BREADSTICKS

■ VEGETARIAN

2 tablespoons active dry yeast

1 tablespoon sugar

1 cup warm water

2 cups brown rice flour

2 cups tapioca flour

½ cup soy flour

¾ cup nonfat dry milk
    powder

1 tablespoon xanthan gum

1 tablespoon garlic powder
    (optional)

1 teaspoon salt

4 tablespoons olive oil

4 large egg whites

½ cup hot water

Olive oil for rolling out dough
    and brushing

Freshly grated Parmesan
    cheese, for sprinkling

1. Preheat the oven to 400°F. Grease a baking sheet with nonstick cooking spray.

2. In a small bowl, combine the yeast and sugar with the warm water and allow to soften for about 5 minutes. You'll know it's ready when the mixture appears to bubble or "bloom."

3. In the bowl of a stand mixer, combine the flours, dry milk powder, xanthan gum, garlic powder, if using, and salt. Blend on the low setting until thoroughly combined.

4. With the mixer running, slowly add the yeast mixture, oil, egg whites, and hot water; mix on medium speed until a smooth dough forms, 5 to 6 minutes.

5. Rub a small amount of oil on your hands and drizzle some on the cutting board. Divide the dough into 4 equal chunks. Roll each portion of dough into a long rope, about ½ inch thick. Cut the breadsticks to the desired length. Place them on the prepared baking sheet and let rest for 15 minutes.

6. Brush a small amount of oil on the top of each breadstick. Sprinkle with cheese. Bake for 12 to 15 minutes, until the cheese begins to turn golden brown.

7. If you have leftover breadsticks, wrap in foil and freeze for up to 3 months.

Tomato-Basil Bisque

A rich soup is the perfect way to start a home-cooked meal. If you don't like tomatoes and basil, you can substitute your favorite vegetable. The rest of the ingredients stay the same, as do the instructions. Try using mushrooms, squash, broccoli, cauliflower, or potatoes.

MAKES
8 SERVINGS

VEGETARIAN

2 tablespoons olive oil

1 yellow onion, diced

Pinch of salt

8 large tomatoes, sliced in quarters

4 cups vegetable stock

½ cup fresh basil leaves

1 tablespoon sugar

1 cup heavy cream

Salt and freshly ground black pepper

1. In a large pot, heat the oil over medium heat. Add the onions and pinch of salt and cook, stirring frequently, until the onions become translucent, 5 to 7 minutes. Add the tomatoes, stock, basil, and sugar and stir well. Bring to a boil, stirring every few minutes. Reduce the heat, cover, and simmer for 20 minutes.

2. Remove from the heat and, using an immersion blender, blend until smooth. (You may also transfer the contents of the pot to a traditional blender to do this, but be careful because the sauce will be hot.) Turn the heat back on to medium and stir in the cream. Simmer for 10 minutes. Season with the salt and pepper and serve.

Tomato, Basil, and Mozzarella with Balsamic Vinegar

This recipe comes from the kitchen of Chef Keith Brunell of Maggiano's Little Italy. Tomato, basil, and mozzarella salad is a classic on the menus of most Italian restaurants. This is an easy, elegant dish to serve at any dinner party. The arrangement and stacking of ingredients works in any fashion; just make it as pretty as possible!

MAKES
4 SERVINGS

■ VEGETARIAN

3 ripe beefsteak tomatoes, sliced

1 teaspoon salt

1 teaspoon freshly ground black pepper

3 fresh mozzarella cheese balls (same size as tomatoes)

1 cup fresh basil leaves

2 tablespoons balsamic vinegar

1. Season the tomato slices with the salt and pepper. In a decorative fan shape, place a slice of cheese, a tomato slice, and then a basil leaf, repeating until all the ingredients are used. Drizzle with the vinegar and serve.

RISOTTOS

Risotto should be its own food group, at least on the food pyramid for people with Celiac Disease! When I was first diagnosed with Celiac, I would always eat tons of salad and never feel full, or I would be hungry again in a few hours. Risotto changed my life. I started simple with just a basic recipe for cooking Arborio rice. I would serve it with chicken or fish and would be thrilled. But as I began experimenting more and more, I found that you can mix anything with risotto! You can add any vegetables and proteins and create delicious sauce bases to flavor the risotto.

I always use Arborio rice when cooking risotto. You can also use Carnaroli rice, but it's more expensive and more difficult to find in stores. Just be sure that you pick rice that has a high starch content. This will ensure a creamy risotto.

Many of these risottos use cheese to give them flavor. Cheese is an amazing ingredient to add, especially those with a strong flavor, like Manchego and goat cheese. If you're on a dairy-free diet, the substitutions are easy: Just replace the cheese in the ingredient list with soy cheese, but be sure to grate it very finely. And, you might want to add a little bit more of the spices and salt to boost the flavors.

For vegetarian substitutions, replace meat or seafood with portabella mushrooms or tofu. You can use the same seasonings and enjoy a delicious gluten-free and meat-free risotto.

Here are some of my favorites. Try them and then see if you can come up with your own combinations using your favorite ingredients!

Artichoke, Sausage, and Mozzarella Risotto

I use chicken or turkey sausage with this risotto. The flavors are subtle add the perfect amount of spice. Many flavored sausages contain gluten, so double-check the ingredients. And use plain artichokes; some marinated ones are not gluten-free.

MAKES
4 SERVINGS

9 tablespoons olive oil

1 pound precooked sausage links, diced (can use chicken or turkey sausage)

2 cups canned artichoke hearts, drained and chopped

½ tablespoon garlic powder

Salt

½ cup diced yellow onion

2 garlic cloves, minced

1½ cups Arborio rice

4 cups chicken stock

1 cup dry white wine

1 cup shredded mozzarella cheese

Salt and freshly ground black pepper

1. In a small saucepan, heat 3 tablespoons of the oil over medium-high heat. Stir in the sausage and cook, stirring, until lightly browned, 6 to 8 minutes. Stir in the artichoke hearts and season with the garlic powder and salt. Cook, stirring frequently, for 5 minutes more. Remove from the heat and set aside.

2. In a medium saucepan, heat 3 tablespoons of the oil over medium-high heat. Add the onions and garlic and cook, stirring, until the onions turn translucent, 5 to 7 minutes. Add the rice and the remaining 3 tablespoons of the oil and cook, stirring constantly, for 2 to 3 minutes.

3. Slowly add the stock, 1 cup at a time, and cook, stirring constantly, allowing the liquid to absorb before adding another cup of the stock. Continue until all the stock is added; this should take 12 to 15 minutes in total.

4. Add the wine and stir well. Add the sausage and artichoke mixture and cook, stirring, until most of the liquid is absorbed, about 5 minutes. Fold in the cheese, stirring gently, until it is fully melted. Add salt and pepper to taste. Allow to cool for 2 to 3 minutes before serving.

● DAIRY-FREE OPTION

Eliminate the cheese or replace it with your favorite soy-based cheese and add a bit more salt. If you use a soy cheese, grate it very finely, or it will not melt evenly.

Grilled Chicken with Asparagus and Cheddar Risotto

Cheddar cheese has a sharp and distinctive flavor that adds a unique richness to risotto. Either white or yellow cheddar will work nicely.

MAKES 4 SERVINGS

FOR THE CHICKEN

4 boneless, skinless chicken breasts (about 1½ pounds total)

2 tablespoons lime juice

1 tablespoon garlic powder

Salt and freshly ground black pepper

FOR THE RISOTTO

6 tablespoons olive oil

½ cup diced yellow onion

2 garlic cloves, minced

2 cups Arborio rice

5 cups chicken stock

1 bunch fresh asparagus, trimmed and chopped into bite-sized pieces

2 cups grated white cheddar cheese

½ cup freshly grated Parmesan cheese

FOR THE CHICKEN

1. Preheat the grill or a grill pan. Pour the lime juice over the chicken breasts and season with the garlic powder, salt, and pepper. Cook the breasts for about 10 minutes on each side, depending on thickness, until fully cooked. Set aside.

FOR THE RISOTTO

1. In a medium saucepan, heat 3 tablespoons of the oil over medium-high heat. Add the onions and garlic and cook, stirring, until the onions turn translucent, 5 to 7 minutes. Add the rice and remaining 3 tablespoons of oil and cook, stirring constantly, for 2 to 3 minutes.

2. Slowly add the stock, 1 cup at a time, and cook, stirring constantly, allowing the liquid to absorb before adding another cup of the stock. After adding 2 cups of the stock, add in the asparagus and cook, stirring, for 4 to 5 minutes. After adding 4 cups of the stock, gently stir in both cheeses. Continue until all the stock is added; this should take 12 to 15 minutes in total. Cook, stirring constantly, until the cheese is fully melted and most of the liquid is absorbed, about 4 to 5 minutes. Add salt and pepper to taste.

3. Allow to cool for 2 to 3 minutes before serving. Serve the chicken breasts on the risotto.

● DAIRY-FREE OPTION

Use a soy-based cheese in place of both the cheddar and Parmesan cheeses.
Be sure to grate the soy cheese extra fine so it melts evenly throughout
the risotto.

● VEGETARIAN OPTION

Replace chicken with large slices of grilled tofu or portabella mushrooms, and
use vegetable stock in place of the chicken stock.

Creamy Parmesan Risotto with Roasted Herb Tomatoes

This is a hearty vegetarian dish. Serve the roasted tomatoes on top of the risotto and allow the flavors to seep into the rice before serving.

MAKES
 4 SERVINGS

VEGETARIAN

4 large tomatoes

Olive oil for drizzling

¼ cup Italian seasoning

Salt and freshly ground black
  pepper

2 cups freshly grated
  Parmesan cheese

6 tablespoons olive oil

½ cup diced yellow onion

2 garlic cloves, minced

1½ cups Arborio rice

5 cups vegetable stock

9 ounces fresh spinach, stems
  removed and roughly
  chopped

1. Preheat the oven to 400°F.

2. Slice the tomatoes in quarters and place on a lightly greased baking sheet. Pour a small amount of oil over the top of each slice. Sprinkle Italian seasoning, salt, and pepper onto each slice. Sprinkle 1 cup of the cheese over the tomatoes. Bake for 15 to 20 minutes or until the cheese browns.

3. Meanwhile, in a medium saucepan, heat 3 tablespoons of the oil over medium-high heat. Add the onions and garlic and cook, stirring, until the onions turn translucent, 5 to 7 minutes. Add the rice and remaining 3 tablespoons of oil and cook, stirring constantly, for 2 to 3 minutes.

4. Slowly add the stock, 1 cup at a time, and cook, stirring constantly, allowing the liquid to absorb before adding another cup of the stock. Continue until all the stock is added; this should take 12 to 15 minutes in total.

5. Gently stir in the remaining 1 cup of Parmesan cheese and the spinach. Cook, stirring gently, until the cheese has fully melted and the spinach is wilted, about 2 minutes.

6. Add salt and pepper to taste. Remove from the heat and spoon the baked tomatoes over the risotto. Allow to cool for 5 minutes before serving.

Creamy Crab and Green Pea Risotto

Crab is a delicacy that can be prepared a number of different ways to showcase its rich flavor. The crab flavor is absorbed throughout this risotto and makes every bite better than the last. Be sure to always use fresh crabmeat. Most imitation crab contains wheat starch as a binder, so it's not gluten-free.

**MAKES
4 SERVINGS**

FOR THE CRAB AND PEAS

2 tablespoons butter

3 cups fresh crabmeat

2 cups frozen green peas, thawed

Salt and freshly ground black pepper

FOR THE RISOTTO

6 tablespoons olive oil

¼ cup chopped shallots

2 garlic cloves, minced

1½ cups Arborio rice

4 cups fish stock or clam juice

1 cup dry white wine

1 cup freshly grated Parmesan cheese

FOR THE CRAB AND PEAS

1. In a small sauté pan, heat the butter over medium-high heat. Add the crabmeat and peas and cook, stirring, until lightly browned, 5 to 7 minutes. Season with the salt and pepper. Remove from the heat and set aside.

FOR THE RISOTTO

1. In a medium saucepan, heat 3 tablespoons of oil over medium-high heat. Add in the shallots and garlic and cook, stirring, until the shallots are lightly browned, 5 to 7 minutes. Add the rice and remaining 3 tablespoons of oil and cook, stirring constantly, for 2 to 3 minutes.

2. Slowly add the stock or juice, 1 cup at a time, allowing the liquid to absorb before adding another cup of the stock. Continue until all the stock is added; this should take 12 to 15 minutes in total.

3. Add in the wine and cook, stirring, until most of the liquid is absorbed, 5 to 6 minutes. Stir in the crab and pea mixture and simmer until most of the liquid is absorbed, 3 to 4 minutes. Gently stir in the cheese and cook until it is fully melted. Add salt and pepper to taste. Allow the risotto to cool for 2 to 3 minutes before serving.

Pesto Risotto with Calamari and Baby Shrimp

I invented this risotto one day when I had a few tablespoons of pesto left over from a previous meal. I didn't want it to go to waste, so I decided use it to to enhance the flavor of my seafood risotto. It turned out to be one of the most delicious risottos I've ever made. The pesto flavors are fresh and light and the perfect complement to the seafood. Buy baby shrimp that are already cleaned, peeled, and deveined.

MAKES
4 SERVINGS

FOR THE PESTO SAUCE

½ pound fresh basil

1 bunch arugula

½ bunch fresh parsley

¼ cup freshly grated Parmesan cheese

2 tablespoons extra-virgin olive oil

Salt and freshly ground black pepper

½ cup pine nuts (optional)

FOR THE PESTO SAUCE

1. In a food processor, combine the basil, arugula, parsley, cheese, and 1 tablespoon of the oil and slowly puree. Make sure everything is chopped, but not pureed into a liquid. If the mixture appears too thick, add the remaining 1 tablespoon of oil. Add salt and pepper to taste. Add the pine nuts, if using, and blend until finely chopped and incorporated. Set aside until needed for risotto.

FOR THE RISOTTO

2 tablespoons butter

1 pound calamari, cleaned
and cut into ½-inch rings

1 pound baby shrimp

1 tablespoon fresh lemon juice

Salt and freshly ground black
pepper

6 tablespoons olive oil

1 cup diced yellow onion

1 tablespoon minced garlic

1½ cups Arborio rice

5 cups chicken stock

¼ cup freshly grated
Parmesan cheese

½ cup pesto sauce

FOR THE RISOTTO

1. In a large sauté pan, melt the butter over medium-high heat. Add the calamari, shrimp, lemon juice, and a pinch of salt and pepper. Cook, stirring occasionally, for 2 to 3 minutes on each side. Set aside.

2. In a medium saucepan, heat 3 tablespoons of the oil over medium-high heat. Add the onions and garlic and cook, stirring, until the onions turn translucent, 5 to 7 minutes. Add the rice and remaining 3 tablespoons of oil and cook, stirring constantly, for 2 to 3 minutes.

3. Slowly add the stock, 1 cup at a time, and cook, stirring constantly, allowing the liquid to absorb before adding another cup of the stock. Continue until all the stock is added; this should take 12 to 15 minutes in total.

4. Add in the seafood mixture and cook, stirring, until well incorporated, 3 to 4 minutes.

5. Gently stir in the cheese and pesto sauce. Stir until the sauce is well mixed in and most of the liquid is absorbed, 3 to 4 minutes. Add salt and pepper to taste.

6. Allow to cool for 2 to 3 minutes before serving.

Seafood Risotto

This recipe comes from the kitchen of Chef Keith Brunell of Maggiano's Little Italy. It is a delightful dish showcasing a traditional meal that people with Celiac Disease can order in an Italian restaurant. The ingredients are naturally gluten-free and blend together to form a succulent risotto.

MAKES
4 SERVINGS

1 tablespoon soybean oil or other vegetable oil

16 medium shrimp, peeled and deveined

Salt and freshly ground black pepper

6 tablespoons olive oil

1 cup diced yellow onion

2 tablespoons minced garlic

1 cup Arborio rice

4 cups clam juice

2 teaspoons ground saffron

2 tomatoes, diced

2 tablespoons chopped basil leaves

3 tablespoons freshly grated Parmesan cheese

1. In a medium sauté pan, heat the oil over medium-high heat. Add the shrimp, season with the salt and pepper, and cook quickly on both sides, stirring frequently, until they are cooked through, about 3 minutes. Set aside.

2. In a medium saucepan, heat 3 tablespoons of the oil over medium-high heat. Add the onions and garlic and cook, stirring, until the onions turn translucent, 5 to 7 minutes. Add the rice and remaining 3 tablespoons of oil and cook, stirring constantly, for 2 to 3 minutes.

3. Slowly add the clam juice, 1 cup at a time, and cook, stirring constantly, allowing the liquid to absorb before adding another cup of the juice. Add in the saffron, tomatoes, and basil, and stir until well incorporated. Continue until all the juice is added; this should take 12 to 15 minutes in total.

4. Gently fold in the cheese and stir until it is fully melted, about 2 minutes. Once the cheese is fully melted and the liquid is absorbed, remove from the heat.

5. Allow to cool for 2 to 3 minutes before serving. Serve the risotto with the shrimp on top.

Portabella and Fresh Spinach Risotto with Goat Cheese Cream

One bite of this creamy risotto—luscious and bursting with flavor—is never enough. You will just keep wanting more.

MAKES
4 SERVINGS

■ VEGETARIAN

6 tablespoons olive oil

4 large portabella mushrooms, diced

1 cup diced yellow onion

2 garlic cloves, minced

1½ cups Arborio rice

5 cups vegetable stock

1 cup grated or crumbled goat cheese (can use smoked goat cheese if desired)

½ cup freshly grated Parmesan cheese

1 pound fresh spinach

Salt and freshly ground black pepper

1. In a medium saucepan, heat 3 tablespoons of the oil over medium-high heat. Add the mushrooms, onions, and garlic and cook, stirring, until the onions turn translucent, 5 to 7 minutes. Add the rice and remaining 3 tablespoons of oil and cook, stirring constantly, for 2 to 3 minutes.

2. Slowly add the stock, 1 cup at a time, and cook, stirring constantly, allowing the liquid to absorb before adding another cup of the stock. Continue until all the stock is added; this should take 12 to 15 minutes in total.

3. Gently stir in both cheeses. Cook, stirring, until the cheese is melted, about 2 minutes. Add the spinach and cook, stirring, until wilted. Add salt and pepper to taste.

4. Allow the risotto to cool for 2 to 3 minutes before serving.

● DAIRY-FREE OPTION

Eliminate the Parmesan and goat cheeses. You can replace them with 2 tablespoons of dairy-free cream cheese. You may want to add a bit more salt, but you will still have a wonderful flavor to your risotto.

Seared Scallops with Zucchini and Manchego Cheese Risotto

Manchego cheese just may be the best cheese on earth. It is made from sheep's milk and comes from the La Mancha region of Spain, just like Don Quixote! It is the perfect blend of creamy and salty and can be enjoyed by itself, on gluten-free crackers, or in risotto with this recipe. Be sure to wait until the very end to use with salt. Manchego cheese is super salty, so you'll want to add it carefully.

MAKES 4 SERVINGS

FOR THE SCALLOPS
16 large scallops

3 tablespoons olive oil

Salt

FOR THE RISOTTO
6 tablespoons olive oil

2 cups diced zucchini

1 cup diced yellow onion

2 garlic cloves, minced

1½ cups Arborio rice

5 cups chicken stock

2 cups grated Manchego cheese

1 cup freshly grated Parmesan cheese

Salt and freshly ground black pepper

FOR THE SCALLOPS

1. Pat the scallops dry with a paper towel. In a medium skillet, heat the oil over medium-high heat. Once the oil is hot, add the scallops to the pan and cook for about 3 minutes, or until you can easily lift a scallop. Flip the scallops over and cook on the opposite side until they are golden brown and can easily be lifted, about 2 to 3 minutes. Remove from the pan and sprinkle a pinch of salt on each scallop. Set aside.

FOR THE RISOTTO

1. In a medium saucepan, heat 3 tablespoons of the oil over medium-high heat. Add the zucchini, onions, and garlic and cook, stirring, until the onions turn translucent, 5 to 7 minutes. Add the rice and remaining 3 tablespoons of oil and cook, stirring constantly, for 2 to 3 minutes.

2. Slowly add the stock, 1 cup at a time, and cook, stirring constantly, allowing the liquid to absorb before adding another cup of the stock. Continue until all the stock is added; this should take 12 to 15 minutes in total.

3. Fold in both cheeses, stirring constantly, until it is fully melted, about 2 minutes. Add salt and pepper to taste.

4. Allow to cool for 2 to 3 minutes before serving. Top each serving with 4 scallops.

▨ VEGETARIAN OPTION

Use vegetable stock in place of chicken stock. You can replace the scallops with grilled portabella mushrooms or any of your other favorite vegetables.

Three-Mushroom, White Wine, and Garlic Risotto

Mushrooms are one of my favorite vegetables. When cooked, they offer a variety of flavors that enhance risotto perfectly. I like to use portabella, crimini, and shiitake mushrooms, but you can use any variety you like.

MAKES
4 SERVINGS

■ VEGETARIAN

6 tablespoons olive oil

2 large portabella mushrooms, sliced thinly

1 cup thinly sliced crimini mushrooms

1 cup thinly sliced shiitake mushrooms

1 cup diced yellow onion

2 garlic cloves, minced

1½ cups Arborio rice

3 cups vegetable stock

2 cups dry white wine

2 cups freshly grated Parmesan cheese

Salt and freshly ground black pepper

1. In a medium saucepan, heat 3 tablespoons of the oil over medium-high heat. Add the mushrooms, onions, and garlic and cook, stirring, until the onions turn translucent, 5 to 7 minutes. Add the rice and remaining 3 tablespoons of oil and cook, stirring constantly, for 2 to 3 minutes.

2. Slowly add the stock, 1 cup at a time, and cook, stirring constantly, allowing the liquid to absorb before adding another cup of the stock. Continue until all the stock is added; this should take 12 to 15 minutes in total.

3. Stir in the wine gradually, allowing time for the liquid to absorb, 4 to 5 minutes.

4. Fold in the cheese, stirring gently, until it is fully melted, about 2 minutes. Add salt and pepper to taste.

5. Allow to cool for 2 to 3 minutes before serving.

● DAIRY-FREE OPTION

Eliminate the Parmesan cheese. You can replace it with soy cheese, but it is almost unnecessary. If you do make the substitution, grate the soy cheese very finely.

Garden Vegetable Risotto

I love eating a plate full of fresh vegetables. But I like them even more when they are part of a risotto. This recipe combines the whole garden into a filling and satisfying gluten-free vegetarian meal.

MAKES
4 SERVINGS

■ VEGETARIAN

7 tablespoons olive oil

1 cup chopped red bell pepper

1 cup diced yellow onion

1 cup diced yellow squash

1 cup diced zucchini

1 cup sliced button mushrooms

2 carrots, peeled and cut into short thin strips

2 garlic cloves, minced

1½ cups Arborio rice

3 cups vegetable stock

2 cups dry white wine

2 cups freshly grated Parmesan cheese

Salt and freshly ground black pepper

1. In a medium saucepan, heat 4 tablespoons of the oil over medium-high heat. Add the bell peppers, onions, squash, zucchini, mushrooms, carrots, and garlic and cook, stirring, until the onions turn translucent, 5 to 7 minutes. Add the rice and remaining 3 tablespoons of oil and cook, stirring constantly, for 2 to 3 minutes.

2. Slowly add the stock, 1 cup at a time, and cook, stirring constantly, allowing the liquid to absorb before adding another cup of the stock. Continue until all the stock is added; this should take 12 to 15 minutes in total.

3. Add in the wine gradually, allowing time for the liquid to absorb, 4 to 5 minutes.

4. Fold in the cheese, stirring gently, until it is fully melted, about 2 minutes. Add salt and pepper to taste.

5. Allow to cool for 2 to 3 minutes before serving.

● DAIRY-FREE OPTION

Eliminate the Parmesan cheese. You may want to add a bit more salt, but you will still have a wonderful flavor to your risotto.

Redbridge Risotto with Asparagus and Red Peppers

Gluten-free beer is an incredible invention for people with Celiac Disease or gluten intolerance. So, why not cook with it? Redbridge is made from sorghum and adds a hearty, full-bodied taste to the risotto. This is a very rich, vegetarian dish! If you eat meat, try serving it with grilled chicken or steak.

MAKES
4 SERVINGS

■ VEGETARIAN

7 tablespoons olive oil

1 bunch asparagus, chopped
   into bite-sized pieces

2 red bell peppers, diced

1 cup diced yellow onion

2 garlic cloves, minced

1½ cups Arborio rice

3 cups vegetable stock

One 12-ounce bottle
   Redbridge gluten-free beer

2 cups grated cheddar cheese

Salt and freshly ground black
   pepper

1. In a medium saucepan, heat 4 tablespoons of the oil over medium-high heat. Add the asparagus, bell peppers, onions, and garlic and cook, stirring, until the onions turn translucent, 5 to 7 minutes. Add the rice and remaining 3 tablespoons of oil and cook, stirring constantly, for 2 to 3 minutes.

2. Slowly add the stock, 1 cup at a time, and cook, stirring constantly, allowing the liquid to absorb before adding another cup of the stock. Continue until all the stock is added; this should take 10 to 12 minutes in total.

3. Stir in the beer gradually, allowing time for the liquid to absorb; do not add the beer too quickly or it may fizz over. Bring to a boil and gently fold in the cheese, stirring constantly until it is fully melted, about 2 minutes. Add salt and pepper to taste.

4. Allow to cool for 2 to 3 minutes before serving. Serve with a bottle of Redbridge beer!

● DAIRY-FREE OPTION

Replace the cheddar cheese with a soy cheese that is grated finely.

PASTAS

Pasta is one of the things I missed the most when I was first diagnosed with Celiac Disease. Don't ever tell my doctors this, but the day I found out I had Celiac, I actually went to an Italian restaurant and ordered a pizza and ravioli. It was my last gluten-containing meal and the last time I thought I would ever eat pasta. Once again I was wrong. Several food manufacturers have started selling gluten-free pastas that taste pretty amazing! My personal favorite is the Tinkyáda brown rice pasta, but there are lots of different types to try. Some use corn as a base, while others use quinoa flour. The pasta recipes that follow are just a starting point. Try these out and then put your own spin on them!

For vegetarian substitutions, replace meat or seafood with large portabella mushrooms or with tofu. You can use the same seasonings and enjoy a delicious gluten-free and vegetarian pasta. Also, be sure to switch to soy milk or vegetable stock in the sauce if you're dairy-free or vegetarian.

Baked Ziti with Sausage

This recipe comes from the kitchen of Chef Keith Brunell of Maggiano's Little Italy. Baked ziti is one of my childhood favorites. It is a perfect meal to satisfy the palates of both adults and children. This version uses a rich Italian sausage.

MAKES
6 SERVINGS

One 1-pound package gluten-free ziti

2 tablespoons olive oil

1 pound sweet Italian sausage, roughly chopped into bite-sized pieces

2 tablespoons minced garlic

1 cup white wine

1 recipe Marinara Sauce (page 31) or 1 quart jarred marinara sauce

1 pound tomatoes, diced

½ cup chopped basil leaves

1 tablespoon butter

2 cups shredded mozzarella cheese

3 tablespoons freshly grated Parmesan cheese

1. In a large pot of salted boiling water, cook the pasta according to the package instructions. Drain and set aside.

2. In a separate large pot, heat the oil over medium-high heat and add the sausage. cooking and stirring for about 10 minutes, until it appears fully cooked.

3. Add the garlic and continue cooking, stirring constantly, for about 2 minutes. Add the wine and cook, stirring, until it is almost completely evaporated. Reduce the heat to medium and add the Marinara Sauce, tomatoes, basil, and butter and cook, stirring frequently, for about 4 to 5 minutes.

4. Remove from the heat and stir in the pasta and half of the mozzarella cheese. Transfer the mixture to a 2-quart glass baking dish, top with the remaining mozzarella cheese, and sprinkle the Parmesan cheese over the top.

5. Preheat the oven broiler and place the ziti underneath the broiler for 3 to 5 minutes, until the cheese is bubbly and golden brown; be sure to watch the ziti carefully to prevent it from burning.

● DAIRY-FREE OPTION

Use soy cheese in place of the mozzarella and Parmesan cheeses.

■ VEGETARIAN OPTION

Replace the sausage with your favorite diced vegetables.

Fettuccine Alfredo with Broccoli

This recipe comes from the kitchen of Chef Keith Brunell of Maggiano's Little Italy. Rich, creamy fettuccine Alfredo is an Italian restaurant classic. Add grilled chicken, mushrooms, or any other protein to make this an even heartier meal.

MAKES
4 SERVINGS

■ VEGETARIAN

One 1-pound package gluten-free fettuccine

2 pounds broccoli, florets (stems discarded or saved for another use)

cup water

1 recipe Alfredo Sauce (page 36)

1. In a large pot of salted boiling water, cook the pasta according to the package instructions. Drain and set aside.

2. While the pasta is cooking, roughly chop the broccoli florets and place them in a microwave-safe bowl. Add $1/2$ cup water and microwave on high heat for 2 minutes. Set aside.

3. In a large sauté pan, combine the Alfredo Sauce and broccoli and cook over medium-low heat, stirring frequently, for 4 to 5 minutes. Add the pasta and stir well.

Garlic Shrimp with Linguine and Roasted Garlic–White Wine Sauce

This recipe comes from the kitchen of Chef Keith Brunell of Maggiano's Little Italy. It is a light and tasty pasta dish perfect for a summer night.

MAKES
4 SERVINGS

One 1-pound package gluten-free linguine

1 tablespoon olive oil

16 medium shrimp, peeled and deveined

Salt and freshly ground black pepper

2 tablespoons minced garlic

½ cup white wine

½ pound diced tomatoes

1 cup clam juice

2 tablespoons chopped basil leaves

1 tablespoon butter

1. In a large pot of salted boiling water, cook the pasta according to the package instructions. Drain and set aside.

2. In a large sauté pan, heat the oil over medium-high heat and add the shrimp. Season with the salt and pepper and cook, stirring, until the shrimp begin to turn pink, about 1 minute. Flip them over, and continue cooking for 1 minute; you do not want the shrimp to be fully cooked. Add the garlic and continue cooking until the garlic is softened, about 1 minute more.

3. Add the wine and bring to a simmer. Cook, stirring frequently, until the wine is reduced by half, about 8 minutes. Add the tomatoes, clam juice, basil, and butter. Bring the sauce to a simmer, stirring, and add in the pasta. Stir well and continue to cook for 2 to 3 minutes. Remove from the heat and season with the salt and pepper.

Beer-Battered Chicken Cutlets with Eggplant and Peas in a Rosemary-Beer Sauce

Beer and rosemary are a fantastic combination, and together they give a wonderful flavor to a pasta sauce.

MAKES 4 SERVINGS

One 1-pound package brown rice penne

1 tablespoon active dry yeast

One 12-ounce bottle Redbridge gluten-free beer

½ cup brown rice flour

½ cup cornstarch

3 tablespoons Italian seasoning

1 tablespoon sugar

4 boneless, skinless chicken breasts (about 1 ½ pounds total)

Vegetable oil, for frying

½ cup olive oil

1 medium eggplant, diced with skin on

1 cup frozen peas, thawed

1 recipe Rosemary-Beer Sauce (page 37)

Salt and freshly ground black pepper

Freshly grated Parmesan cheese, for serving

1. In a large pot of salted boiling water, cook the pasta according to the package instructions. Drain and set aside.

2. In a medium bowl, dissolve the yeast in the beer for about 5 minutes, until the mixture bubbles, or "blooms." Add the flour, cornstarch, Italian seasoning, and sugar and whisk together well. Dip the chicken breasts into the batter and coat well.

3. In a large skillet, heat the vegetable oil over medium-high heat and fry the chicken until cooked through, about 8 minutes on each side.

4. While the chicken cooks, in a separate large skillet, heat the olive oil over medium-high heat. Add the eggplant and peas and cook, stirring, until the eggplant softens, 6 to 8 minutes. Add the Rosemary-Beer Sauce and bring to a simmer. Gently stir in the pasta and season with the salt and pepper. Cook 3 minutes more. Set aside until the chicken is ready.

5. Slice chicken and place on top of the pasta. Serve with Parmesan cheese.

VEGETARIAN OPTION

This dish can be made vegetarian simply by eliminating the chicken.

Portabella and Pea Macaroni and Cheese

One day I was trying to use up a bunch of ingredients in my refrigerator, I tossed a variety of vegetables together and melted several different cheeses into a sauce. It was amazing! This is a more refined version. If you're allergic to potato starch, you can replace it with cornstarch.

MAKES
4 SERVINGS

▦ VEGETARIAN

One 1-pound package gluten-free elbow macaroni

¼ cup butter

2 cups thickly sliced portabella mushrooms

1 cup frozen green peas, thawed

2 cups milk

1 cup dry white wine

1 tablespoon potato starch

2 cups grated sharp cheddar cheese

½ cup freshly grated Parmesan cheese

1 teaspoon paprika

Salt

1. In a large pot of salted boiling water, cook the pasta according to the package instructions. Drain and set aside.

2. In a medium skillet, melt the butter over medium-high heat. Add the mushrooms and peas and cook, stirring, until lightly browned. Set aside.

3. In a medium saucepan, combine the milk and wine. Bring the mixture to a boil, stirring occasionally. In a small bowl, mix the potato starch with 1 tablespoon of water to make a paste. Pour the paste into the milk and wine mixture and cook, stirring rapidly, until the sauce thickens.

4. Slowly stir in the cheeses and cook, stirring, until they are fully melted, about 2 minutes. Stir in the paprika.

5. In a large serving bowl, combine the pasta, cheese sauce, and vegetables. Add salt to taste.

Pasta with Sausage, Spinach, Mushrooms, and Asparagus in Cabernet-Garlic Sauce

This is a very colorful dish. I typically use turkey or chicken sausage, but any variety will work just fine. I like to use penne pasta, but choose your favorite gluten-free variety.

**MAKES
4 SERVINGS**

One 1-pound package gluten-free pasta

6 tablespoons olive oil

1 cup diced yellow onion

1 tablespoon minced garlic

1 pound sweet Italian sausage, roughly chopped into bite-sized pieces

8 ounces button mushrooms, sliced

1 bunch asparagus, trimmed and roughly chopped

3 cups loosely packed fresh spinach

1 recipe Cabernet-Garlic Sauce (page 35), heated

Salt

1. In a large pot of salted boiling water, cook the pasta according to the package instructions. Drain and set aside.

2. In a large sauté pan, heat 3 tablespoons of the oil over medium-high heat. Add the onions and garlic and cook, stirring, until lightly browned, 5 to 7 minutes. Add the sausage and cook until about halfway cooked. Add the remaining 3 tablespoons of oil, the mushrooms and asparagus and cook, stirring, until the mushrooms are lightly browned, 5 to 6 minutes. Add the spinach and cook, stirring, until it is wilted.

3. Slowly pour the Cabernet-Garlic Sauce over the vegetables and simmer for 5 minutes.

4. Season with the salt and serve over the pasta.

Seafood Pasta in a Creamy Parmesan Broth

Seafood and pasta were made to go together . . . at least in my opinion! This light and creamy dish is perfect for any dinner party. Your guests will be impressed. I like to use spaghetti in this dish, but pick any pasta variety and it will taste delicious.

**MAKES
4 SERVINGS**

One 1-pound package gluten-free pasta

6 tablespoons olive oil

½ cup diced yellow onion

2 garlic cloves, minced

8 large scallops, chopped into small pieces

1 pound medium shrimp, peeled and deveined

1 tablespoon cornstarch

3 cups chicken stock (or 2 cups chicken stock and 1 cup white wine)

1 head broccoli, chopped

2 cups freshly grated Parmesan cheese

1 tablespoon Italian seasoning

½ teaspoon salt

½ teaspoon freshly ground black pepper

Freshly grated Parmesan cheese, for serving

1. In a large pot of salted boiling water, cook the pasta according to the package instructions. Drain and set aside.

2. In a large sauté pan, heat the oil over medium-high heat. Add the onions and garlic and cook, stirring, until lightly browned, 5 to 7 minutes. Add the scallops and shrimp and cook, stirring frequently, for about 3 minutes. Add the cornstarch and stir well until the liquids thicken, about 1 to 2 minutes.

3. Add the stock and broccoli and cook, stirring, until a thick sauce forms, 5 to 6 minutes. Gently stir in the cheese, Italian seasoning, salt, and pepper and simmer for about 5 minutes.

4. Place the pasta into a large serving bowl and pour the seafood mixture over it. Toss gently. Serve with additional cheese.

Spaghetti with Cherry Tomato Sauce

Try garnishing this simple, light, and elegant dish with fresh parsley.

MAKES
4 SERVINGS

● DAIRY-FREE

▦ VEGETARIAN

One 1-pound package gluten-
  free spaghetti

1 recipe Cherry Tomato Sauce
  (page 38), heated

1. In a large pot of salted boiling water, cook the pasta according to the package instructions. Drain and set aside.

2. In a large bowl, combine the pasta and Cherry Tomato Sauce. Toss well before serving.

Spaghetti with Meat Sauce and Sausage

This recipe comes from the kitchen of Chef Keith Brunell of Maggiano's Little Italy. It is a rich dish that will satisfy the heartiest eater!

MAKES
4 SERVINGS

● DAIRY-FREE

One 1-pound package gluten-free spaghetti

3 tablespoons olive oil

1 pound sweet Italian sausage links, roughly chopped into bite-sized pieces

1 tablespoon minced garlic

Salt and freshly ground black pepper

1 recipe Meat Sauce (page 32), heated

1. In a large pot of salted boiling water, cook the pasta according to the package instructions. Drain and set aside.

2. In a large sauté pan, heat the oil over medium-high heat. Add the sausage and garlic and cook, stirring, until the sausage is lightly browned on all sides, 8 to 10 minutes. Season with the salt and pepper.

3. In a large bowl, combine the pasta, sausage, and Meat Sauce. Stir well before serving.

Turkey Meatballs with Vodka Sauce

Meatballs are one of those foods you wouldn't expect to be made with gluten. But most restaurants use breadcrumbs to hold the balls together. This recipe substitutes potato starch and Parmesan cheese. If you're allergic to potato starch, you can replace it with cornstarch. Use your favorite brand of vodka for the sauce. Although rumors say there is gluten in vodka, the distillation process removes all traces of the gluten protein, making it a safe ingredient for cooking—and drinking!

MAKES 4 SERVINGS

One 1-pound package gluten-free pasta

1 pound ground turkey

3 large eggs

1 cup freshly grated Parmesan cheese

¼ cup potato starch

2 garlic cloves, minced

1 teaspoon dried basil

1 teaspoon dried oregano

1 teaspoon kosher salt

1 recipe Vodka Sauce (page 40), heated

Freshly grated Parmesan cheese, for serving

1. In a large pot of salted boiling water, cook the pasta according to the package instructions. Drain and set aside.

2. Preheat the oven to 350°F. Grease a baking sheet with nonstick cooking spray.

3. In a large bowl, combine the turkey and eggs. Add the cheese, potato starch, garlic, basil, oregano, and salt. Mix together well.

4. Form the meat mixture into 2-inch balls. Place the balls on the prepared baking sheet and bake for 15 minutes. Turn the balls over and bake for 15 minutes more.

5. In a large bowl, slowly and gently fold the cooked meatballs into the Vodka Sauce. Let the meatballs sit for about 5 minutes before serving to absorb some of the sauce.

6. On a serving plate, ladle the meatballs and sauce onto the pasta and serve with additional cheese.

MAIN DISHES

These main dishes are the ones that make my mouth water the most! And, of course, the recipes you crave the most will be the most difficult to make, or at least to make using gluten-free alternatives. They are breaded, utilize flour, and require you to make dough out of flours. Since there is no good one-to-one gluten-free substitution for regular flour, you have to use a blend of different flours including tapioca flour, brown rice flour, white rice flour, soy flour, potato starch, and cornstarch. But don't worry! Just follow these recipes closely and you'll be able to make the most delicious gluten-free versions of each of these specialties.

There are many different flours used in the recipes here. Several different vendors make these flours, but I personally choose to use Bob's Red Mill brand, mainly because the company certifies its products as gluten-free. They have a dedicated mill for gluten-free flours and grains, meaning that I never need to worry about cross- contamination.

Chicken Parmesan

Chicken Parmesan combines the best textures of crispy breading and perfectly cooked pasta. This breading is a perfect gluten-free substitute! Serve with Marinara Sauce and a side of gluten-free spaghetti.

MAKES
4 SERVINGS

One 1-pound package gluten-free spaghetti

2 tablespoons olive oil

3 garlic cloves, minced

Salt

4 boneless, skinless chicken breasts (about 1½ pounds total)

2 large eggs, beaten

2 teaspoons Italian seasoning

1 cup freshly grated Parmesan cheese

¾ cup brown rice flour

¾ cup cornstarch

Canola oil, for frying (enough to submerge the chicken breasts halfway)

Freshly grated Parmesan cheese for sprinkling (see # 4)

1 recipe Marinara Sauce (page 31), heated

1. In a large pot of salted boiling water, cook the pasta according to the package instructions. Drain and set aside.

2. In a small bowl, combine the oil, garlic, and salt and whisk together well. Rub the mixture onto the chicken breasts and allow to sit for about 5 minutes. In a separate bowl, whisk together the eggs and Italian seasoning. In a third bowl, combine the cheese, flour, and cornstarch, and mix together well. Dip each chicken breast into the egg mixture and then immediately into the dry ingredients, coating the chicken well.

3. In a large skillet, heat the oil over medium-high heat and cook the chicken until golden brown, about 8 minutes on each side.

4. Remove the chicken from the oil and immediately top each piece with additional cheese.

5. Fill four plates with pasta. Place a piece of chicken on the pasta and top with a large spoonful of the Marinara Sauce.

◼ VEGETARIAN OPTION

For a vegetarian dish, replace the chicken with eggplant, for eggplant Parmesan.

Turkey-Spinach Lasagne

Before I was diagnosed with Celiac Disease, lasagna was one of my favorite foods. When I'd make it—by popular demand—for a dinner party, my friends and family would take leftovers home. All that changed after my diagnosis, until I discovered Tinkyáda brown rice noodles; they taste just like the real thing, don't get mushy or stick together, and are the right size!

**MAKES
6 SERVINGS**

One 1-pound package Tinkyáda brown rice lasagna noodles

2 tablespoons olive oil

1 pound ground turkey (can substitute ground chicken or beef)

1 yellow onion, diced

4 tablespoons ketchup

2 tablespoons minced garlic

1 pound fresh spinach

Salt and freshly ground black pepper

8 ounces ricotta cheese

½ cup freshly grated Parmesan cheese

1 large egg

2 tablespoons Italian seasoning

1 recipe Marinara Sauce (page 31)

6 cups shredded mozzarella cheese

1. Preheat the oven to 375°F.

2. In a large pot of salted boiling water, cook the pasta according to the package instructions. Drain and set aside.

3. In a large skillet, heat the oil over medium-high heat. Add the turkey, onions, ketchup, and garlic, and cook, stirring, until the turkey is fully cooked and the onions are lightly browned, 8 to 10 minutes. Add the spinach and cook, stirring, until wilted. Season with the salt and pepper and remove from the heat. Set aside until ready for assembly.

4. In a small bowl, combine the ricotta cheese, Parmesan cheese, egg, 1 tablespoon of the Italian seasoning, and a pinch of salt. Stir together well.

5. In the bottom of a 9 x 13-inch glass baking dish, spread ½ cup of the Marinara Sauce. Place 3 lasagna noodles over the sauce. Spread the turkey and spinach mixture evenly over the noodles. Pour a small amount of the sauce on top. Sprinkle with 2 cups of the mozzarella cheese. Add another layer of 3 lasagna noodles, and spread the ricotta mixture over them; sprinkle with 2 cups of the mozzarella cheese. Add a final layer of 3 more lasagna noodles. Pour the remaining sauce on top and allow the sauce to seep through the layers. Sprinkle on the remaining 2 cups of the mozzarella cheese and top with the remaining 1 tablespoon of Italian seasoning.

6. Cover the baking dish with foil and bake for 20 minutes. Remove the foil and bake for 25 minutes more, until the cheese is bubbly and golden brown.

Pizza Crust

You can roll this crust out thick or thin, and either way you'll have a pizza crust that looks, smells, and tastes like it came out of your favorite pizzeria!

■ VEGETARIAN

2 tablespoons active dry yeast

1 tablespoon sugar

1 cup warm water

2½ cups brown rice flour

1 cup tapioca flour

½ cup soy flour

¾ cup nonfat dry milk powder

1 tablespoon xanthan gum

1 teaspoon salt

½ cup hot water

4 tablespoons olive oil

4 large egg whites

Olive oil, for rolling out dough

1. Preheat the oven to 400°F. Grease a circular pizza pan with nonstick cooking spray.

2. In a small bowl, combine the yeast and sugar with the warm water and allow to soften for about 5 minutes. You'll know it's ready when the mixture appears to bubble, or "bloom."

3. In the bowl of a stand mixer, combine the flours, dry milk powder, xanthan gum, and salt. Blend on the low setting until thoroughly mixed. With the mixer running, slowly add the yeast mixture, hot water, oil, and egg whites and mix on medium speed until a smooth dough forms, 5 to 6 minutes.

4. Coat your hands with oil. Move the dough to the prepared pan and spread and press into a large, thin pizza shell, about ½ inch thick. Allow the crust to rise for 15 minutes.

5. Transfer the crust to the oven and bake for 5 to 7 minutes. Remove the crust from the oven and add your favorite toppings. Cook 15 minutes more, or until the cheese turns golden brown.

Ideas for Pizza Toppings

- Marinara Sauce (page 31), pepperoni, mushrooms, and mozzarella cheese

- Marinara Sauce (page 31), pineapple, mushrooms, onions, and mozzarella cheese

- Marinara Sauce (page 31), green bell peppers, onions, olives, and mozzarella cheese

- Marinara Sauce (page 31), basil, sliced tomatoes, and mozzarella cheese

- Pesto Sauce (page 33), sun-dried tomatoes, and goat cheese

- Pesto Sauce (page 33), mushrooms, artichoke hearts, and mozzarella cheese

- Alfredo Sauce (page 36), sweet Italian sausage, olives, and Parmesan cheese

- Alfredo Sauce (page 36), grilled chicken, broccoli, tomatoes, and Parmesan cheese

- Alfredo Sauce (page 36), caramelized onions, spinach, mushrooms, and mozzarella cheese

Stromboli

Stromboli is bread at its best! This is a delicious dough that I like to fill with fresh mozzarella cheese and kosher salami. But you can put whatever ingredients you would like inside the stromboli.

MAKES
4 SERVINGS

2 tablespoons active dry yeast

1 tablespoon sugar

1 cup warm water

2½ cups brown rice flour

1 cup tapioca flour

½ cup soy flour

¾ cup nonfat dry milk powder

1 tablespoon xanthan gum

1 teaspoon salt

4 tablespoons olive oil

4 large egg whites

½ cup hot water

Olive oil for rolling out dough and brushing

2 cups shredded mozzarella cheese

6 ounces salami, sliced thinly

Marinara Sauce (page 31) or Pesto Sauce (page 33), for dipping

1. Preheat the oven to 400°F. Grease a baking sheet with nonstick cooking spray.

2. In a small bowl, combine the yeast and sugar with the warm water and allow to soften for about 5 minutes. You'll know it's ready when the mixture appears to bubble, or "bloom."

3. In the bowl of a stand mixer, combine the flours, dry milk powder, xanthan gum, and salt. Blend on the low setting until thoroughly mixed.

4. With the mixer running, slowly add the yeast mixture, oil, egg whites, and hot water and mix on medium speed until a smooth dough forms, 5 to 6 minutes.

5. Cover a surface, your hands, and a rolling pin with oil. Move the dough to the greased surface. The dough will be very sticky, so using the well-greased rolling pin, roll dough into a large rectangle, about 11 inches long and 14 inches wide.

6. Lightly dust the baking sheet with brown rice flour and move the dough onto it. Cover the surface of the dough with the cheese and salami. Gently roll the stromboli up from the bottom to the top along the 14-inch side. Pinch the ends together tightly. Brush the outside with oil.

7. Bake for 20 to 25 minutes. Remove from the oven and slice before serving. Serve with the Marinara Sauce or Pesto Sauce for dipping.

▦ VEGETARIAN OPTION

Try using just cheese or adding fresh vegetables instead of the salami.

Calzones

This is my fancy version of a favorite meal from childhood. Fill the calzones with what you like best. I favor mushrooms, onions, zucchini, mozzarella cheese, and Marinara Sauce inside, but the fillings are up to you! You can even make all eight calzones with different ingredients in each, perfect for a dinner party where your guests all have different preferences.

2 tablespoons active dry yeast

1 tablespoon sugar

1 cup warm water

2½ cups brown rice flour

1 cup tapioca flour

½ cup soy flour

¾ cup nonfat dry milk powder

1 tablespoon xanthan gum

1 teaspoon salt

½ cup hot water

4 large egg whites

4 tablespoons olive oil

Olive oil, for rolling out dough and brushing

2 cups shredded mozzarella cheese

1 cup diced yellow onion

1 cup diced zucchini

1 cup thinly sliced portabella mushrooms

1 cup Marinara Sauce (page 31), plus 1 to 2 cups extra for dipping (optional)

1. Preheat the oven to 400°F. Grease a baking sheet with nonstick cooking spray.

2. In a small bowl, combine the yeast and sugar with the warm water and allow to soften for about 5 minutes. You'll know it's ready when the mixture appears to bubble, or "bloom."

3. In the bowl of a stand mixer, combine the flours, the dry milk powder, xanthan gum, and salt. Blend on the low setting until thoroughly mixed.

4. With the mixer running, slowly add the yeast mixture, hot water, egg whites, and oil; mix on medium speed until a smooth dough forms, 5 to 6 minutes.

5. Oil your hands and workspace and divide the dough into 8 equal-sized balls. Using a rolling pin, roll each ball into a circle 5 to 6 inches in diameter. Divide the cheese, onions, zucchini, mushrooms, and Marinara Sauce evenly among the 8 circles, keeping the filling on one side. Do not over-stuff.

6. Fold the dough over to create a pocket. Seal the edges tightly. Move the calzones onto the prepared baking sheet and brush the outer layer of the dough with oil and cut small slits in the top for ventilation. Bake for 20 to 25 minutes and serve with Marinara Sauce for dipping, if desired.

Eggplant Pizza and Mushroom Pizza Caps

This is the simplest way to make pizza that you'll ever find! The eggplant and mushrooms make the pizza super healthy and save you the time of having to make a crust. And it tastes divine.

MAKES
4 SERVINGS

■ VEGETARIAN

1 large eggplant

4 large portabella mushroom caps

2 cups Marinara Sauce (page 31)

1 teaspoon Italian seasoning

Salt and freshly ground black pepper

3 cups shredded mozzarella cheese

Optional toppings: pepperoni, onions, bell peppers, mushrooms, fresh tomatoes, roasted red peppers, pine-apple, ham, basil—use your imagination!

1. Preheat the oven to 350°F. Grease a baking sheet with nonstick cooking spray. Cut the ends off the eggplant and slice it lengthwise into ½-inch thick slices and lay them on the baking sheet. Lay the mushroom caps next to the eggplant.

2. Cover each slice to its edges with the Marinara Sauce. Add the Italian seasoning, salt, and pepper.

3. Top the eggplant and mushroom slices with the cheese and your favorite optional toppings. Bake for 10 to 15 minutes, until the cheese is bubbly and lightly browned.

Eggplant Rollatini

This is one of my childhood favorites. It's a bit strange that a kid liked eggplant, but I just couldn't get enough! I love the way the flavor of ricotta cheese goes with the eggplant, and the soft texture the eggplant gets when it's baked is sublime.

MAKES
4 SERVINGS

■ VEGETARIAN

3 medium eggplants

¼ cup extra-virgin olive oil

2 large eggs

32 ounces ricotta cheese

1 cup freshly grated Parmesan cheese

1 cup shredded mozzarella cheese

Salt and freshly ground black pepper

1 recipe Marinara Sauce (page 31)

1. Preheat the oven to 375°F. Grease a 2-quart baking dish with oil.

2. Cut the ends off the eggplant and slice it lengthwise into ½-inch thick slices. Place the eggplant slices on a large baking sheet and lightly drizzle with the oil. Bake for 10 minutes.

3. In a large bowl, beat the eggs gently and then mix in the ricotta and Parmesan cheeses and ½ cup of the mozzarella cheese.

4. Remove the eggplant from the oven and cool. Place about 2 tablespoons of the cheese mixture on one end of each eggplant slice. Roll up the slices and place them in the prepared baking dish. Season with salt and pepper. Top the eggplant generously with the Marinara Sauce and sprinkle the remaining ½ cup of mozzarella cheese on top. Bake for 15 minutes. Allow to cool for 2 to 3 minutes before serving.

Beef Medallions with Garlic Mashed Potatoes and Spinach

Everyone will be impressed when you serve this complex, high-quality dinner. You could get a reputaion for being a champion chef!

MAKES 4 SERVINGS

FOR THE BEEF

1 pound beef tenderloin

Salt and freshly ground black pepper

4 tablespoons butter

FOR THE GARLIC MASHED POTATOES

8 red potatoes

4 garlic cloves

¼ cup milk

¼ cup sour cream

2 tablespoons olive oil

1 cup freshly grated Parmesan cheese

1 teaspoon kosher salt

1 teaspoon freshly ground black pepper

FOR THE SPINACH

¼ cup olive oil

1 tablespoon minced garlic

1 pound fresh spinach

Salt

FOR THE BEEF

1. Cut the beef into 4 pieces. Season each side with salt and pepper. In a large skillet, melt the butter and add the beef. Cook until both sides are lightly browned, while the center remains pink, about 4 minutes on each side, depending on the thickness of the meat.

FOR THE GARLIC MASHED POTATOES

1. Bring a large pot of water to a boil. Cook the potatoes and garlic for about 20 minutes, or until tender. Drain, then place the potatoes and garlic in a large bowl.

2. Add in the milk, sour cream, and oil and mash together using a potato masher or electric mixer until creamy. Fold in the cheese, salt, and pepper. Keep the potatoes warm.

FOR THE SPINACH

1. In a large skillet, heat the oil over medium-high heat. Add the garlic and cook, stirring, until lightly browned. Add the spinach and cook, stirring, until wilted. Season with the salt.

TO SERVE

1. Spoon a large portion of the spinach onto each plate. Top with a beef medallion. Serve the mashed potatoes on the side.

● DAIRY-FREE OPTION

Eliminate the milk, sour cream, and Parmesan cheese from the mashed potatoes and add ¼ cup plain soy milk and ¼ cup tofu-based sour cream.

Chicken Piccata

This recipe comes from the kitchen of Chef Keith Brunell of Maggiano's Little Italy. It's a light and fresh dish that I order often when visiting Maggiano's. With just a simple change to rice flour, the original dish becomes fabulously gluten-free. This goes well with mashed potatoes or steamed rice.

MAKES
4 SERVINGS

3 tablespoons freshly grated
  Parmesan cheese

3 tablespoons rice flour

4 boneless, skinless chicken
  breasts (about 1 pounds
  total)

3 tablespoons olive oil

1 cup chicken stock

 cup white wine

1 tablespoon capers

1 tablespoon chopped fresh
  basil

1 tablespoon fresh lemon juice

1 teaspoon freshly grated
  lemon zest

4 cups loosely packed fresh
  baby spinach

1 tablespoon butter

Salt and freshly ground black
  pepper

1. In a medium bowl, combine the cheese and flour and coat each piece of chicken with the mixture. In a large skillet, heat 1 tablespoon of the oil over medium-high heat. Carefully place the chicken into the pan. Cook it on one side until golden brown, 7 to 8 minutes, then flip over and continue cooking until golden brown on the other side, 7 to 8 minutes more. Remove the chicken from the pan and set aside.

2. In the same skillet, turn the heat up to high, add the stock and wine, stir up any bits from the bottom of the pan, and cook until the liquid is reduced by half, 7 to 8 minutes. Add the capers, basil, lemon juice, and lemon zest and cook, stirring frequently, for 5 to 7 minutes. Return the chicken to the pan, bring the sauce to a simmer, and add the butter, stirring continuously until it is completely melted.

3. Meanwhile, in a medium sauté pan, heat the remaining 2 tablespoons of oil over medium-high heat. Add the spinach and cook, stirring, until wilted. Season with the salt and pepper and place the spinach on a serving plate.

4. Place the chicken on the spinach and pour the sauce over the chicken for serving.

Chicken Marsala

This recipe comes from the kitchen of Chef Keith Brunell of Maggiano's Little Italy. Garlic mashed potatoes (page 85) would be the ideal complement to the rich and nuanced flavor of mushrooms, butter, and wine.

MAKES
4 SERVINGS

3 tablespoons rice flour

3 tablespoons freshly grated Parmesan cheese

4 boneless skinless chicken breasts (about 1 pounds total)

1 tablespoon olive oil

1 cup sliced button mushrooms

cup diced onion

1 teaspoon minced garlic

cup Marsala wine

1 cup beef stock

1 tablespoon butter

1 tablespoon chopped fresh basil

1 tablespoon chopped fresh parsley

1. In a large bowl, combine the flour and grated cheese and dust each piece of chicken with the mixture. In a large skillet, heat the oil over medium-high heat. Carefully place the chicken into the pan. Cook the chicken on one side until golden brown, 5 to 6 minutes, then flip it over and continue cooking until golden brown on the other side, 5 to 6 minutes more. Remove from the pan and set aside.

2. In the same pan, combine the mushrooms, onions, and garlic, and cook, stirring, until the onions are softened, 4 to 5 minutes. Add the wine and simmer until almost dry. Add the stock, bring to a simmer, and cook until reduced by half, about 8 minutes.

3. Place the chicken back into the pan. Add the butter, basil, and parsley and cook, stirring continuously, until the butter has completely melted. Remove the chicken from the pan and place it on a plate. Pour the sauce over the chicken for serving.

Salmon Cakes with Dill-Yogurt Sauce

These cakes are a variation of a salmon loaf that my grandma made when I was a little girl. This version is simple, eliminates breadcrumbs, and tastes amazing! If you're allergic to potato starch, you can replace it with cornstarch. The cakes work well by themselves or on gluten-free buns.

**MAKES
4 SALMON CAKES**

FOR THE SALMON

1 pound skinless salmon fillets, diced

1 large egg, beaten lightly

2 scallions, finely diced

3 tablespoons potato starch

1 teaspoon freshly grated lemon zest

1 tablespoon fresh lemon juice

1 tablespoon white horseradish

Salt and freshly ground black pepper

FOR THE DILL-YOGURT SAUCE

½ cup plain yogurt

2 tablespoons finely chopped fresh dill

1 teaspoon salt

1 teaspoon freshly ground black pepper

FOR THE SALMON

1. Preheat the oven broiler. Line a baking sheet with foil and grease with oil.

2. In a large bowl, combine the salmon, egg, scallions, potato starch, lemon zest, lemon juice, and horseradish. Mix together well.

3. Form the salmon mixture into 4 equal-sized cakes and place on the prepared baking sheet. Season the top of the cakes with the salt and pepper. Broil for 8 to 10 minutes, or until the cakes are browned on top.

FOR THE DILL-YOGURT SAUCE

1. Meanwhile, in a small bowl, combine the yogurt, dill, salt, and pepper and mix well. Serve with the salmon cakes.

● **DAIRY-FREE OPTION**

Use dairy-free plain yogurt.

Gnocchi with Vodka Sauce

Did you know that most store-bought gnocchi contain wheat flour? Not these! A few simple substitutions make homemade gnocchi that are gluten-free and fabulous. If the gnocchi mixture is too watery, just add a bit more brown rice flour to thicken it.

MAKES
4 SERVINGS

VEGETARIAN

2 pounds whole baking
  potatoes
2 cups brown rice flour
½ cup tapioca flour
2 teaspoons xanthan gum
2 large eggs, beaten
1 teaspoon salt
1 recipe Vodka Sauce
  (page 40), heated

1. Preheat the oven to 350°F.

2. Spear the potatoes in several places with a fork to allow moisture to vent. Place them on a baking sheet and bake for 1 hour. Cut open the potatoes and allow them to cool for about 20 minutes. Scoop the potato out of the skins and put it through a potato ricer. If you don't have a ricer, don't worry; just mash the potato by hand using a fork.

3. Add the flours, xanthan gum, eggs, and salt to the potatoes and mix together to form a ball of dough.

4. Dust a cutting board with brown rice flour. Break off a small piece of dough and roll it into a rope 1-inch in diameter. Cut the ropes into 1-inch-long pieces. Repeat until all the dough is cut. Place the cut gnocchi on a flour–dusted baking sheet. Freeze the gnocchi on the sheet for about 1 hour. After the gnocchi are frozen, you can store them in a resealable plastic bag up to 1 month in the freezer or cook them.

5. To cook the gnocchi, in a large pot bring 5 quarts of salted water to a boil. Gently add the frozen gnocchi. Cook until the gnocchi rise to the surface of the water, about 5 minutes. Drain the gnocchi and serve topped with the Vodka Sauce.

● DAIRY-FREE OPTION
Substitute Marinara Sauce (page 31) for the Vodka Sauce.

Spinach Gnocchi with Gorgonzola Cream Sauce

This is a spiced-up version of traditional gnocchi. Be sure to dry the spinach well and drain the potatoes thoroughly before mixing them together. If the mixture is watery, add additional brown rice flour to thicken it. Also, you can substitute cornstarch for the potato starch if you are allergic.

MAKES
4 SERVINGS

■ VEGETARIAN

FOR THE SPINACH GNOCCHI

1 pound whole baking potatoes

12 ounces frozen spinach, thawed, patted dry, and chopped

8 ounces ricotta cheese

2 large eggs, beaten

2 cups brown rice flour

½ cup tapioca flour

1 tablespoon garlic powder

1 tablespoon potato starch

1 tablespoon xanthan gum

1 teaspoon salt

FOR THE SPINACH GNOCCHI

1. Preheat the oven to 350°F.

2. Spear the potatoes in several places with a fork to allow moisture to vent. Place them on a baking sheet and bake for 1 hour. Cut open the potatoes and allow them to cool for about 20 minutes. Scoop the potato out of the skins and put it through a potato ricer. If you don't have a ricer, don't worry; just mash the potatoes by hand using a fork.

3. In a large bowl, combine the spinach, cheese and potatoes and stir well. Add the eggs, flours, garlic powder, potato starch, xanthan gum, and salt and mix together to form a ball of dough.

4. Dust a cutting board with brown rice flour. Break off a small piece of dough and roll it into a rope 1-inch in diameter. Cut the ropes into 1-inch-long pieces. Repeat until all the dough is cut. Place the cut gnocchi on a flour-dusted baking sheet. Freeze the gnocchi on the sheet for about 1 hour. After the gnocchi are frozen, you can store them in a resealable plastic bag up to 1 month in the freezer or cook them.

5. To cook the gnocchi, in a large pot bring 5 quarts of salted water to a boil. Gently add the frozen gnocchi. Cook until the gnocchi rise to the surface of the water, about 5 minutes. Drain.

FOR THE GORGONZOLA CREAM SAUCE

2 cups heavy cream

¼ cup white wine

½ cup crumbled Gorgonzola cheese

Salt and freshly ground black pepper

FOR THE GORGONZOLA CREAM SAUCE

1. In a small saucepan, bring the cream and wine to a gentle simmer over medium heat, stirring constantly. Remove from the heat and stir in the cheese. Season with the salt and pepper. Pour the gorgonzola cream sauce over the gnocchi and serve immediately.

● DAIRY-FREE OPTION

Substitute Marinara Sauce (page 31) or Pesto Sauce (page 33) for the gorgonzola cream sauce.

Asian
GLUTEN-FREE
COOKING

FROM CHEF
Katie Chin
of Thai Kitchen
author of *Everyday Chinese Cooking*

Asian cuisine has become extremely popular among Americans of all ages because of the amazing flavors, textures, and cooking methods that this diverse cuisine has to offer. Asian cuisine has something for everyone: from the harmonious blend of colors and flavors in Chinese stir-fries and the fiery heat of Indonesian dishes to the sweet, salty, sour, and spicy allure of Thai and Vietnamese cooking—Asian dishes excite the senses.

Every Asian region has a distinct flavor and personality. The first dietary culture of Asia is the Northeast tradition, comprising China, Korea, and Japan. Arguably, Chinese cuisine has become the most prominent of all Asian styles of cooking, with several different styles based on each region—the most basic difference being between northern and southern styles. Southern dishes emphasize freshness and subtle flavors as well as the use of steaming, roasting, and stir-frying. Due to the colder weather, northerners are known for heartier fare with strong flavors such as moo shu pork and the abundance of noodles and dumplings. In contrast, Japanese cooking came to emphasize the frequent use of deep-frying such as tempura and raw foods (sushi and sashimi). In Korea, much of the traditional cuisine is centered on grilling or sautéing and the use of chiles, spices, and condiments—for example, kim chi.

The second major dietary culture of Asia is the Southeast style, which includes the foods of Thailand, Laos, Cambodia, Vietnam, Indonesia, Malaysia, Singapore, and Brunei. The traditional emphasis in this region is on aromatic and lightly prepared foods, using a delicate balance of quick stir-frying, steaming, and boiling. The prominent flavors of Southeast Asia are sweet, hot, sour, and salty. Fish sauce, citrus juices, and herbs such as basil, cilantro, and mint as well as lemongrass and turmeric are commonly used in Southeast Asian cuisine.

I love to take my family and friends on a culinary tour of these exotic destinations every time I cook. The great thing about Asian cuisine is that you can turn an everyday meal into an everyday adventure.

My friends have told me that they feel as if they've been transported to a market in China with ducks blowing in the wind every time I make tea-smoked duck or like they're sitting on a beach in Thailand dipping their toes in the water when I treat them to a mango shake and refreshing Thai lettuce wraps.

There are five basic cooking techniques used in Asian cooking: stir-frying, steaming, deep-frying, grilling, and pan-frying. Because most of the dishes are cooked quickly over a high flame with little oil, Asian cuisine can be extremely healthy. Many recipes call for a rainbow of colorful vegetables, and I always encourage people to experiment and try new varieties of Asian vegetables.

Due to the popularity of Asian cuisine, many supermarkets now carry Asian produce, such as bok choy and edamame. However, you don't have to use Asian vegetables. Just as long as you use fresh ingredients, you really can't go wrong! When my mother immigrated to Minnesota from China, she couldn't even find garlic at the market. She improvised, using the vegetables in our garden, and we were treated to delectable slices of beef dancing in velvety gravy among the fresh tomatoes and basil from our backyard.

It's also very easy to cook Asian dishes on a regular basis as long as you have the right staple ingredients on hand in your pantry. I recommend keeping the following items on hand for everyday Asian cooking: ginger, garlic, fish sauce, hoisin sauce, oyster sauce, rice noodles, chili sauce, dried Thai chiles, Jasmine rice, vinegar, cornstarch, curry paste, lemongrass, soy sauce, and coconut milk.

These staple ingredients will enable you to capture the subtle and delicate flavors in a Cantonese stir-fry one night and create a sour and spicy Thai soup the next. Knowing the basic techniques and flavors will give you the confidence to improvise and blend these methods and tastes together. The beautiful thing about Pan-Asian cuisine is that all of the flavors complement one another, so home chefs can serve a variety of sweet, salty, sour, and hot flavors together. From teriyaki and pad Thai, to lo mein and Vietnamese spring rolls—there are limitless options for everyday menu planning and entertaining.

When designing an Asian-inspired menu, I always try to remember the ancient yin and yang philosophy of cooking. Asian people believe that a balance of yin (cool, tranquil, feminine) energy and yang (warm, active, masculine) energy in all aspects of life will lead to a harmonious existence. Food and cooking are no exception. It is believed that every ingredient has either a yin (cooling) or yang (heating) quality. For example, most vegetables, fish, and tofu have cool-ing, yin qualities while meat, eggs, and spicy foods are considered very yang, with heat. To achieve a balanced diet, Asians strive to choose a menu that includes some yang dishes complemented by yin dishes. There-fore, a typical Asian meal might include a steamed fish and vegetable dish balanced harmoniously with a spicy beef with ginger recipe.

Asian cuisine is also excellent for left-overs. For example, I took some shrimp that I grilled the other night and mixed it with chilled rice noodles, spring greens, and some peanut sauce. In five minutes, I had an authentic and refreshing Southeast Asian salad for lunch. I also love to take shredded roast chicken from the market to create a wonderful Asian noodle soup with rice noo-dles, ginger, cilantro, pea pods, and sesame oil. It turns an average lunch into a tantaliz-ing treat for my family's taste buds.

Asian cuisine also has numerous health benefits. Ginger is known to aid in digestion and ease stomach cramps. I love to steep some fresh ginger in hot water whenever I have a tummy ache. Turmeric is considered to be one of nature's most powerful natural healers, proving beneficial in the treatment of cancer and Alzheimer's Disease. Mean-while, chiles and coconut milk have proven to help one's heart run smoothly. Coconut milk is also an excellent milk substitute for the lactose and casein intolerant. Next time you're feeling under the weather, you should try some lemongrass, as it's been used for centuries to fight off colds and the flu. Tofu and edamame have also been touted as soy champions, reducing heart disease. Last but not least, green tea is an antioxidant powerhouse. No wonder people living in Asia tend to live longer and have fewer diseases. Now, we can all drink to that!

Another amazing benefit of Asian cuisine is that most of the ingredients that are used are naturally gluten-free, creating an array of choices for people with Celiac Disease.

In Asia rice is abundant because the grain is easy to grow in warm climates. It is inexpensive to grow, and millions can be fed on very little money. In fact, three billion people depend on rice to survive. Humid climates make it difficult for wheat production and, therefore, Asian countries developed rice-based diets instead of bread and potatoes.

As rice is the main ingredient and staple food of the Asian diet, it's only natural that other products would be born out of Asians' love of rice. Rice flour, made of crushed rice,

is the basis for rice noodles and rice paper. Rice noodles are extremely versatile and can be boiled, steamed, or fried. Rice paper wrappers are excellent for making chilled Vietnamese summer rolls, but they can also be steamed for making gluten-free wontons and dumplings.

Tofu is a terrific source of protein and is also naturally gluten-free. In Asian markets you can even find tofu that has been stretched and shaped like pasta. It has a similar consistency to noodles, but is wheat-free and full of protein.

People living with Celiac Disease can take advantage of the versatility of rice and tofu in their diets. I recently cooked a dinner for a friend with Celiac Disease, and she was amazed at all the wonderful dishes I created that were naturally gluten-free. First, I used rice paper to make yummy shrimp and mint summer rolls as an appetizer. I then used chilled rice noodles to make a spicy Thai beef salad. Next, I used some rice noodles in a delicious seafood soup. The entrées included a chicken chow fun dish that used broad, flat rice noodles, a tofu stir-fry, a steamed whole fish with black bean sauce, and shrimp fried rice.

She absolutely loved not worrying about what she was eating and that there was such a variety in terms of textures and flavors.

I know that many people living with Celiac Disease often miss enjoying dishes with sauces because they are often thickened with flour. In Asian cooking, sauces are generally thickened with cornstarch, so people can satisfy their craving for creamy, velvety sauces with delicious Asian stir-fry dishes and stews.

Because of the lack of wheat in many Asian regions, Asians typically use rice flour, tapioca starch, and potato starch. These can be found in Asian markets. It's wonderful to experiment with these ingredients to make dumplings such as gluten-free potstickers. Once you've mastered the dough, you can experiment with a variety of fillings.

Of course, you don't have to venture out to an ethnic market when you feel like cooking Asian. There are now a variety of Asian products that are naturally gluten-free available at your local grocery stores. Thai Kitchen makes a wonderful line of products

that are 100 percent gluten-free and incredibly easy to keep on hand (www.thaikitchen. com).

Here are a few of Thai Kitchen's products that I just love to keep in my pantry: stir-fry rice noodle kits, instant rice noodle soup bowls, rice noodle carts, jasmine rice mixes, dried rice noodles, coconut milk, hot and sour and coconut ginger soups, chili sauces, fish sauce, pad Thai sauce, peanut satay sauce, curry pastes, and simmer sauces.

As you can see, Thai Kitchen's array of products helps create effortless gluten-free cooking as well as ready-to-eat convenience with tremendous variety. Thai Kitchen products are also clearly marked "gluten free" to put your mind at ease while shopping.

Asian cuisine can be part of your everyday routine whether or not you're on a gluten-free diet. With all the wonderful and convenient options available today, home cooks can master the art of Asian cooking and take their friends and family on amazing culinary adventures in no time at all.

Happy cooking!

ASIAN INGREDIENTS *to Keep in Your Kitchen*

There are so many fragrant and flavorful spices involved in Asian cooking. Here are some of the staple Asian ingredients and the items most commonly used in the upcoming recipes. Many of these ingredients have very long shelf lives, so you can stock them in your pantry for use at any time.

SPICES

I always purchase McCormick spices (www.mccormick.com). It is a company policy to always declare on the label if any one of twelve allergens is used in their products, including wheat. If there is no declaration on the package, the only ingredient in the container is the pure spice.

Chili powder

Curry powder

Coconut milk (I always buy Thai Kitchen brand because they certify it is gluten-free.)

Fish sauce (I always buy Thai Kitchen brand because they certify it is gluten-free.)

Garlic powder

Ground ginger

Oils:

Peanut oil

Sesame oil

Vegetable oil

Stock:

Chicken stock (Swanson's is certified gluten-free.)

Vegetable stock

NOODLES AND RICE

I generally only buy Thai Kitchen brand rice noodles and jasmine rice. They certify all of these items as gluten-free and produced in a clean facility.

Jasmine rice

Short grain Sushi rice

Stir-fry rice noodles

Thin rice noodles

SOY SAUCE

There are several brands of soy sauce that are certified gluten-free. Many of the gluten-free brands are much saltier than wheat-based soy sauces, so try a few to find the one that you like best. Here are my favorites.

Eden organic tamari soy sauce

La Choy lite soy sauce

La Choy soy sauce

Panda brand low sodium gluten-free soy sauce (comes in small packets)

San-J organic wheat free reduced sodium tamari soy sauce

San-J organic wheat free tamari soy sauce

CURRY PASTE

I always buy curry paste from Thai Kitchen because they state clearly on the label that their products are gluten-free.

Green curry paste

Red curry paste

OTHER INGREDIENTS

It's not hard to fill one's pantry with common items that can be useful for cooking Asian food. These are some of my favorites to keep around, but when it comes to vegetables, proteins, and nuts, you can choose your favorites and season them with your favorite Asian spices.

Cashews

Chicken, beef, and seafood

Cornstarch

Eggplant

Fresh ginger

Garlic

Green tea

Peanut butter

Pineapple

Potatoes

Rice paper

Thai Kitchen sweet chili sauce (the best for dipping)

Tofu

SOUPS, SALADS, AND STARTERS

One of the things I missed the most when I was diagnosed with Celiac Disease was being able to order take-out Asian food, especially the appetizers. Most of them are fried or use ingredients that contain gluten. As I started investigating various Asian ingredients, I found that almost every food item I loved had a gluten-free option. Rice paper wrappers can be substituted for egg rolls, and gluten-free soy sauce easily replaces the varieties that contain wheat.

Tom Yum Hot and Sour Soup

This recipe comes from the kitchen of Chef Katie Chin. It is a variation on a spicy Asian classic.

MAKES
4 SERVINGS

● DAIRY-FREE

3 cups chicken or vegetable stock

⅓ cup fresh lime juice

2 to 3 tablespoons fish sauce

2 tablespoons sugar

3 pieces fresh lemongrass (tender bottom ⅔ inch of stalk only)

2 kaffir lime leaves (optional)

One 1-inch piece fresh galangal (Thai ginger) or regular ginger, sliced

2 tablespoons Thai Kitchen roasted red chili paste

12 ounces boneless, skinless chicken breasts, cut into large pieces

One 15-ounce can straw mushrooms, drained

Sprigs of fresh cilantro, for garnish (optional)

1. In a large pot, combine the stock, lime juice, fish sauce, sugar, lemongrass, lime leaves, and galangal. Bring to a boil over high heat, then reduce the heat, cover, and simmer for 15 minutes.

2. Add the chili paste and stir well to incorporate. Add the chicken and mushrooms and simmer until the chicken is cooked, 10 to 15 minutes. (If using shrimp or tofu, simmer 10 minutes more before adding them to the soup. Cook until the shrimp turns orange-pink or the tofu is tender, 1 to 2 minutes.)

3. Remove the lemongrass, lime leaves, and galangal from the soup before serving. Garnish with cilantro, if desired.

■ VEGETARIAN OPTION

Replace the chicken with firm tofu.

Coconut-Ginger Soup

A creamy soup to warm you up.

MAKES
4 SERVINGS

● DAIRY-FREE

1 tablespoon peanut oil

2 cups loosely packed fresh
spinach

1 cup shiitake mushrooms,
sliced thinly

½ cup chopped scallions

2 tablespoons grated fresh
ginger

3 cups chicken stock

2 tablespoons fish sauce

Two 14-ounce cans coconut
milk

1 tablespoon chili powder

½ tablespoon cornstarch

Salt and freshly ground black
pepper

1. In a large pot, heat the oil over medium-high heat. Add the spinach, mushrooms, scallions, and ginger and cook, stirring, until the spinach begins to wilt, 1 to 2 minutes.

2. Add 2½ cups of the stock and the fish sauce and stir well. Bring to a boil and add the coconut milk and chili powder. Cook, stirring well, for 3 to 4 minutes.

3. In a small bowl, combine the remaining ½ cup of the stock and the cornstarch and stir until smooth. Slowly pour the mixture into the soup and stir well. Cook until the desired thickness is reached, 10 to 15 minutes. Add salt and pepper to taste.

Asian Noodle Soup

This recipe comes from the kitchen of Chef Katie Chin. It is a delicious noodle soup perfect for any meal, but especially when you are feeling under the weather. It is simple to make and will soothe your soul!

MAKES
4 SERVINGS

● DAIRY-FREE

3 ounces Thai Kitchen thin rice noodles (about 1½ cups cooked)

1 cup shredded cooked chicken

4 cups chicken stock

1 cup water

¼ cup thinly shredded peapods

¼ cup sliced mushrooms

½ teaspoon sesame oil

2 thin slices fresh ginger

Pinch ground white pepper, or to taste

2 tablespoons coarsely chopped fresh cilantro, for garnish

1. In a large pot, bring 8 cups of water to a boil. Add the rice noodles and cook until softened, 3 to 4 minutes. Drain and rinse with cold water. Shake off the excess water and set aside. Divide the noodles into 4 bowls. In each bowl, place an even amount of the chicken over the noodles.

2. In a medium pot, combine the stock, water, peapods, mushrooms, oil, and ginger and bring to a boil. Add the pepper.

3. Pour even amounts of soup into each bowl. Garnish with cilantro and serve immediately.

Seafood Soup

This recipe comes from the kitchen of Chef Katie Chin. The strong flavors pair perfectly with the seafood.

MAKES
4 SERVINGS

● DAIRY-FREE

3 ounces Thai Kitchen thin rice noodles (about 1½ cups cooked)

6 ounces skinless fresh fish fillets, such as sea bass or halibut

1 teaspoon cornstarch

1 teaspoon salt

½ teaspoon sesame oil

2 thin slices fresh ginger

Pinch ground white pepper

4 cups chicken stock

2 cups sliced bok choy

12 ounces large shrimp, peeled, deveined, and cooked

1 scallion with top, minced, for garnish

1. In a large pot, bring 8 cups of salted water to a boil. Add the rice noodles and cook until softened, 3 to 4 minutes. Drain and rinse with cold water. Shake off the excess water and set aside.

2. Rinse the fish fillets in cold water and pat them dry. Cut the fish into thin slices. In a bowl large enough to hold the fish, mix together the cornstarch, salt, oil, ginger, and pepper. Add the fish, stir to coat, and set aside.

3. In a large saucepan, bring the stock to a boil. Add the noodles and return to a boil. Add the bok choy and boil for 1 minute. Add the fish slices, return the soup to a boil, and stir the fish gently to separate the pieces.

4. Add the shrimp and return to a boil for 20 seconds; turn off the heat. Pour into bowls and garnish with scallions.

Egg Drop Soup

A staple of most Asian restaurants that can easily be made at home.

MAKES
4 SERVINGS

● DAIRY-FREE

▦ VEGETARIAN

4 cups vegetable stock

2 scallions with tops, finely minced

1 teaspoon freshly ground black pepper

1 teaspoon salt

1 tablespoon cornstarch

3 large eggs, beaten

1. In a medium saucepan, combine 3 cups of the stock, the scallions, pepper, and salt and bring to a boil.

2. In a small bowl, combine the remaining 1 cup of the stock and the cornstarch and stir until smooth.

3. While rapidly stirring, slowly pour the eggs into the pot of boiling stock, then immediately, while still stirring, slowly pour in the cornstarch mixture. Cook, stirring, until the desired thickness is reached.

Chicken-Lettuce Wraps

This is my favorite appetizer to order at an Asian restaurant. I love the cool crispness of the lettuce and the way it meshes perfectly with the warm filling. You can make the recipe as is, or add chili flakes or chili powder to spice it up.

MAKES
4 SERVINGS

● DAIRY-FREE

4 tablespoons vegetable oil

1 cup diced yellow onion

1 tablespoon minced garlic

1 pound ground chicken (can use ground turkey or beef)

½ cup chopped fresh cilantro

½ cup chopped scallions

½ cup chopped water chestnuts

2 tablespoons fish sauce

2 tablespoons gluten-free soy sauce, plus extra for serving

1 teaspoon chili flakes

1 teaspoon salt

1 teaspoon freshly ground black pepper

8 large iceberg lettuce leaves

1. In a large wok or skillet, heat the oil over medium-high heat. Add the onions and garlic and cook, stirring, until lightly browned, 5 to 7 minutes. Add the chicken and cook, stirring, until the meat is cooked and no pink spots remain, 8 to 10 minutes.

2. Add the cilantro, scallions, water chestnuts, fish sauce, soy sauce, and chili flakes and cook, stirring constantly, for 3 minutes. Season with the salt and pepper.

3. Using the lettuce leaves as cups, fill each with a heaping spoonful of meat mixture. Serve with additional soy sauce.

Crunchy Vietnamese Spring Rolls

This recipe comes from the kitchen of Chef Katie Chin. The crispy spring rolls are naturally gluten-free and filled with amazing flavors. I love dipping them in Thai Kitchen sweet chili sauce. It is certified gluten-free and has a unique tangy taste.

MAKES
12 SPRING ROLLS

● DAIRY-FREE

½ cup cellophane noodles

6 dried Chinese mushrooms

1 pound ground lean pork

¼ cup finely chopped yellow onion

2 small carrots, finely grated

2 garlic cloves, finely chopped

2 large eggs, lightly beaten

1 tablespoon Thai Kitchen premium fish sauce

1 teaspoon salt

1 teaspoon freshly ground black pepper

12 (8½-inch) round rice paper wrappers

2 cups vegetable oil, for frying

Thai Kitchen sweet chili sauce, for dipping

1. In separate medium bowls, soak the noodles and mushrooms in hot water for 30 minutes. Drain the noodles and mushrooms thoroughly. Cut the noodles into 1-inch lengths and finely chop the mushrooms. In a bowl, combine the noodles with the pork, onions, carrots, garlic, eggs, fish sauce, salt, and pepper.

2. Spread a damp clean towel on a counter. Fill a pan with hot water. (Keep a bowl of hot water next to the pan and towel, as you will need to occasionally refill the pan with water.) Arrange all the ingredients within reach.

3. In the pan of hot water, dip one sheet of rice paper to wet it completely. Set the wet paper on the damp towel; the rice paper should become soft and pliable immediately. Fold up the bottom third of the rice paper. Put 1 generous teaspoon of filling in the center of the folded-up portion and press it into a compact rectangle. Fold one side of the rice paper over the mixture, then the other side. Roll from bottom to top to completely enclose the filling. Continue until all the filling is used.

4. In a large wok or skillet, heat the oil to 375°F. Fry the rolls a few at a time, turning occasionally, until crisp, 6 to 8 minutes. Drain on paper towels and serve with the sweet chili sauce, for dipping.

Shrimp and Mint Summer Rolls

This recipe comes from the kitchen of Chef Katie Chin. Summer rolls are a light appetizer filled with seductive flavors. The mint leaves give the perfect kick, and the dipping sauce is a fantastic addition.

MAKES 12 ROLLS, OR ABOUT 6 SERVINGS

● DAIRY-FREE

FOR THE DIPPING SAUCE

¼ cup fresh lime juice

¼ cup sugar

¼ cup Thai Kitchen premium fish sauce

1 teaspoon minced Thai chiles (or to taste, optional)

1 garlic clove, minced

3 tablespoons finely shredded carrots

¼ cup warm water

FOR THE ROLLS

2 ounces Thai Kitchen thin rice noodles, (about 1 cup cooked)

12 (8½-inch) round rice paper wrappers

12 large shrimp, peeled, deveined, cooked, and cut in half lengthwise

FOR THE DIPPING SAUCE

1. In a medium bowl, combine the lime juice, sugar, fish sauce, chile, and garlic and stir until the sugar is dissolved. Stir in the carrots. Add the warm water as needed to dilute.

FOR THE ROLLS

1. In a large pot, bring 6 cups of salted water to a boil. Cook the rice noodles until softened, 2 to 4 minutes. Drain and rinse with cold water. Shake off the excess water and set aside.

2. Spread a damp clean towel on a counter. Fill a pan with hot water. (Keep a bowl of hot water next to the pan and towel, as you will need to occasionally refill the pan with water.) Arrange all the ingredients within reach.

3. In the pan of hot water, dip one sheet of rice paper to wet it completely. Set the paper on the damp towel; the rice paper should become soft and pliable immediately. Arrange 2 pieces of shrimp in a horizontal line on the bottom third (2½ inches from the bottom and 1 inch from right-hand side) of the rice paper wrapper. Place a small portion of rice noodles over the shrimp. Distribute some cucumber, carrots, and 4 to 5 mint leaves over the noodles. Place one lettuce leaf over the mint leaves. Fold the bottom half of the rice paper wrapper over filling, while using your fingers to

1 cup peeled seedless cucumber, sliced into thin strips

¼ cup carrots, sliced into thin strips

¼ cup fresh mint leaves

12 pieces fresh green leaf lettuce (3 by 5 inches), cut along the rib and rib removed

press down on the ingredients. Fold the right-hand side of the rice paper over to enclose the ingredients at the bottom of the roll.

4. Pressing gently on the ingredients with your fingers, tuck in the ends, and gently roll the rice paper up tightly to form a cylinder. Repeat these steps to make the remaining spring rolls. Serve immediately with the dipping sauce.

Golden Fried Tofu

This recipe sounds difficult (and I always thought it *was* difficult when I would order it at restaurants), but it is actually very simple to make. The entire recipe takes about fifteen minutes from start to finish. I like to make extra and save the leftovers for lunch the next day. Also, consider making extra tofu to use in fried rice or pad Thai. This is great served with steamed rice or over vegetables.

MAKES 12 PIECES OF TOFU, OR ABOUT 4 SERVINGS

● DAIRY-FREE

▨ VEGETARIAN

FOR THE DIPPING SAUCE

¼ cup gluten-free soy sauce

1 tablespoon sesame oil

1 teaspoon minced garlic

½ teaspoon chili flakes

FOR THE TOFU

14 ounces extra-firm tofu, drained well

¼ cup brown rice flour

¼ cup cornstarch

1 teaspoon salt

6 cups vegetable oil, for frying

FOR THE DIPPING SAUCE

1. In a small bowl, whisk together the soy sauce, sesame oil, garlic, and chili flakes. Set aside.

FOR THE TOFU:

1. Press paper towels onto the tofu to absorb as much moisture as possible. Cut the tofu into 12 equal-sized pieces.

2. In a small bowl, mix together the flour, cornstarch, and salt. Dip the tofu pieces in the mixture and coat well.

3. In a large skillet, heat the vegetable oil over medium-high heat; it's hot enough when you can see small bubbles in the oil. Add the tofu and fry until lightly browned, about 5 minutes. Flip over each piece of tofu and continue to fry until lightly browned, about 5 minutes more. Serve with the dipping sauce.

Papaya-Mango-
Cucumber Salad

A fresh and light Asian salad. You can serve this in a lettuce-leaf cup or alone on a small plate.

MAKES
4 SERVINGS

● DAIRY-FREE

▨ VEGETARIAN

1 large papaya

1 large mango, ripe but firm
  (slightly green)

1 cucumber

2 tablespoons gluten-free soy
  sauce

1 tablespoon grated fresh
  ginger

1. Peel and thinly slice the papaya, mango, and cucumber into noodle-like shreds.

2. Transfer to a large bowl. Add the soy sauce and ginger and stir well.

Southeast Asian Salad with Grilled Shrimp

This recipe comes from the kitchen of Chef Katie Chin. It's a light and crunchy salad with a fresh taste!

MAKES
4 SERVINGS

● DAIRY-FREE

1 pound medium shrimp, peeled and deveined

3 ounces Thai Kitchen thin rice noodles (about 1½ cups cooked)

6 cups shredded mixed lettuces (romaine, Bibb or baby greens)

½ cup Thai Kitchen peanut sauce

¼ cup mixture of minced fresh cilantro and mint, for garnish

1. Preheat the grill or a grill pan. Cook the shrimp until opaque, about 2 to 3 minutes per side.

2. In a large pot, bring 8 cups of water to a boil. Add the rice noodles and cook until softened, 3 to 4 minutes. Drain and rinse with cold water. Shake off the excess water and set aside.

3. Place the cooked noodles in a large salad bowl and toss with the shrimp, lettuce, and peanut sauce. Garnish with the cilantro and mint.

Thai Beef Salad

This recipe comes from the kitchen of Chef Katie Chin. The beef has a delightful heat that goes perfectly with the crisp lettuce and the clean flavors of the dressing. If you can't find bird's-eye chiles, replace them with a serrano chile.

MAKES
4 SERVINGS

● DAIRY-FREE

FOR THE DRESSING

¼ cup fresh lime juice

¼ cup Thai Kitchen premium fish sauce

4 teaspoons minced garlic

4 teaspoons sugar

2 teaspoons minced bird's-eye chiles

FOR THE SALAD

2 tablespoons gluten-free soy sauce

2 tablespoons vegetable oil

1 teaspoon freshly ground black pepper

8 ounces beef sirloin

¼ cup sliced yellow onion

1 tomato, cut into ¼-inch slices

½ cup sliced cucumber

3 tablespoons sliced (1-inch pieces) scallions with tops

4 large iceberg lettuce leaves (optional)

FOR THE DRESSING

1. In a small bowl, mix together the lime juice, fish sauce, garlic, sugar, and chile. Set aside.

FOR THE SALAD

1. In a large bowl, combine the soy sauce, oil, and pepper. Add the beef, toss to coat, and marinate for about 30 minutes.

2. Preheat the grill or a grill pan and cook the beef to the desired doneness, about 3 to 4 minutes per side for medium-rare. Slice the beef into long, thin strips.

3. In a large bowl, toss together the beef strips and the onions, tomatoes, cucumber, scallions, and dressing. Serve on salad plates, or using the lettuce leaves as cups, fill each with a heaping spoonful of meat mixture.

Potstickers

This recipe comes from the kitchen of Chef Katie Chin. These dumplings are truly amazing. Making gluten-free potsticker dough is no easy task, and this recipe succeeds brilliantly! You can replace the pork with ground beef, chicken, or even crumbled tofu. Also, if you're allergic to potato starch, you can replace it with cornstarch.

MAKES 32 TO 36 DUMPLINGS

● DAIRY-FREE

FOR THE DIPPING SAUCE
¼ cup gluten-free soy sauce
1 teaspoon sesame oil

FOR THE DOUGH
1 cup tapioca flour
½ cup cornstarch
¼ cup sorghum flour
¼ cup potato starch
2 tablespoons xanthan gum
6 large eggs
¼ cup olive oil
1 teaspoon salt

FOR THE DIPPING SAUCE
1. In a small bowl, mix together the soy sauce and sesame oil. Set aside.

FOR THE DOUGH
1. In a medium bowl, combine the tapioca flour, cornstarch, sorghum flour, and potato starch. Add the xanthan gum and stir until well blended.

2. Add the eggs, olive oil, and salt. Stir very well, then use your hands to mix the dough completely. If the dough is too wet, add more potato starch, but don't add so much that it gets stiff and hard. Cover the dough and set aside.

8 ounces Napa cabbage

3 teaspoons salt

1 pound lean ground pork

¼ cup finely chopped
  scallions

1 tablespoon white wine

1 tablespoon cornstarch

1 tablespoon sesame oil

Pinch ground white pepper

2 to 4 tablespoons vegetable
  oil

1. Cut the cabbage crosswise into thin strips. In a large bowl, toss the cabbage with 2 teaspoons of the salt and set aside for 5 minutes. Squeeze out any excess moisture.

2. In a separate large bowl, mix together the cabbage, pork, scallions, wine, cornstarch, the remaining 1 teaspoon of salt, 1 teaspoon of the sesame oil, and the pepper.

3. Divide the dough in half. Shape each half into a rope 12 inches long, and cut each rope into ½-inch slices. Roll 1 slice of the dough into a 3-inch circle and place 1 tablespoon of the filling in the center. Pull up the edges of the circle and pinch up 5 pleats to create a pouch to enclose the filling. Pinch the top together. Repeat with the remaining slices of dough and filling.

4. Heat a large wok or nonstick skillet over high heat until very hot. Add 1 tablespoon of the vegetable oil, tilting the wok to coat the sides. (If you're using a nonstick skillet, add only ½ tablespoon oil.) Place 12 dumplings in a single layer in the wok and fry until the bottoms are golden brown, about 2 minutes. Add ½ cup water, cover, and cook until the water is absorbed, 6 to 7 minutes. Repeat with the remaining dumplings.

5. Serve the dumplings with the dipping sauce.

Crispy Chicken Drumsticks

This recipe is a twist on my mom's fried chicken recipe. You get a subtle hint of ginger and soy in every bite.

MAKES 12
DRUMSTICKS

● DAIRY-FREE

2 cups (or enough to
   submerge the drumsticks
   halfway) vegetable or
   canola oil, for frying

3 large eggs

½ cup gluten-free soy sauce

¼ cup honey

½ cup cornstarch

½ cup brown rice flour

1 tablespoon garlic powder

1 tablespoon ground ginger

2 teaspoons salt

12 chicken drumsticks
   (or chicken legs)

1. Preheat the oven to 350°F.

2. In a large skillet, heat the oil over medium-high heat; it's ready when you see small bubbles in it.

3. In a small bowl, whisk together the eggs, soy sauce, and honey. In a separate small bowl, mix together the cornstarch, flour, garlic powder, ginger, and salt.

4. Dip the drumsticks in the egg mixture. Dip the wet drumsticks into the dry mixture and coat well. Fry the drumsticks in the oil, until lightly browned, about 5 minutes on each side. Remove the drumsticks from the oil and place them on a baking sheet. Bake for 15 minutes, or until the chicken is cooked through.

RICE AND NOODLES

I am always immediately drawn to rice and noodle dishes within every cuisine. I love the way the noodles and rice balance out the other ingredients and make the dishes filling. These rice and noodle recipes are some of my favorite classic Asian dishes that I've reinvented by adding various ingredients such as pineapple and mango. These recipes are easy to make and are great to prepare on a night when you don't have a lot of time for cooking. The other great thing about these dishes is that the bases are naturally gluten-free. Asian restaurants traditionally use rice noodles and rice for their dishes, so the only changes to gluten-free alternatives come within sauces.

Thai Fried Rice

I like to use onions, carrots, peas, and corn when I make this basic Thai fried rice. Use your favorite ingredients to customize the recipe.

MAKES
4 SERVINGS

● DAIRY-FREE

1½ cups jasmine rice

5 tablespoons vegetable oil

3 large eggs, beaten

1 cup diced yellow onion

2 tablespoons minced garlic

1 cup diced carrots

1 cup frozen green peas, thawed

1 cup frozen yellow corn kernels, thawed

3 tablespoons fish sauce

2 tablespoons gluten-free soy sauce

1 tablespoon salt

1 tablespoon freshly ground black pepper

2 cups cooked chicken, beef, or tofu (optional)

½ cup finely chopped scallions, for garnish

1. Cook the rice according to the package instructions. Allow to cool for at least 2 hours before making the fried rice. (You should have 3 cups of cooked rice.)

2. In a large wok or skillet, heat 1 tablespoon of the oil over medium heat, tilting the pan to coat the sides. Add the eggs to the wok and cook, stirring, until cooked through, 5 to 7 minutes. Shred or break up the scrambled eggs and set aside.

3. In the same wok, heat 3 tablespoons of the oil. Add the onions and garlic and cook, stirring frequently, until translucent, 5 to 7 minutes. Add the carrots, peas, and corn and cook, stirring frequently, until softened, 3 to 4 minutes.

4. Stir in the cooked rice, fish sauce, soy sauce, salt, pepper, and the remaining 1 tablespoon of the oil. Cook, stirring constantly, until the rice begins to brown, 5 to 6 minutes. Stir in the cooked eggs.

5. Serve in bowls with the chicken, beef, or tofu, if desired. Garnish with chopped scallions.

Shrimp Fried Rice

This recipe comes from the kitchen of Chef Katie Chin. It is her wonderful version of the always popular shrimp fried rice.

MAKES
4 SERVINGS

● DAIRY-FREE

1½ cups jasmine rice

1½ teaspoons salt

Pinch ground white pepper

2 medium eggs, lightly beaten

2 tablespoons vegetable oil

2 tablespoons gluten-free soy sauce

2 cups peeled, deveined, and diced shrimp

½ cup frozen peas, thawed and patted dry

½ cup small button mushrooms

2 scallions with tops, chopped

1. Cook the rice according to the package instructions. Allow to cool for at least 2 hours before making the fried rice. (You should have 3 cups of cooked rice.)

2. In a medium bowl, add ½ teaspoon of the salt and the pepper to the eggs. Heat a large wok or skillet over high heat until very hot. Add 1 tablespoon of the oil and tilt the wok to coat the sides. Add the eggs and cook, stirring, until the eggs are thickened throughout but still moist, about 2 to 3 minutes. Remove the eggs and set aside. Shred or break up the scrambled eggs. Wash and thoroughly dry the wok.

3. Make sure all the ingredients are dry before cooking. Reheat the wok over high heat until very hot. Add the remaining 1 tablespoon of the oil and tilt to coat the sides of the wok. Add the rice and cook, stirring, for 2 minutes. (If you cannot stir-fry fast enough, reduce the heat so the rice will not burn.)

4. Stir in the soy sauce and continue stirring until mixed well with the rice. Stir in the cooked eggs, shrimp, peas, mushrooms and the remaining 1 teaspoon of the salt. Cook, stirring, until the entire mixture is hot, about 2 minutes. Stir in the scallions.

Mango Fried Rice

Everyone will love this fantastic dish. The mango lends the perfect sweet note to the mellow rice. Prepare the recipe as is, or add in chicken or tofu for a more filling dish.

● DAIRY-FREE
■ VEGETARIAN

1½ cups jasmine rice

5 tablespoons vegetable oil

3 large eggs, beaten

2 cups chopped fresh mango (about 2 mangoes)

1 cup diced carrots

1 cup diced yellow onion

1 cup frozen green peas, thawed

1 cup frozen yellow corn kernels, thawed

2 tablespoons minced garlic

½ cup finely chopped scallions

3 tablespoons fish sauce

3 tablespoons gluten-free soy sauce

1 tablespoon fresh lime juice

Salt and freshly ground black pepper

1. Cook the rice according to the package instructions. Allow to cool for at least 2 hours before making the fried rice. (You should have 3 cups of cooked rice.)

2. In a large wok or skillet, heat 1 tablespoon of the oil over medium heat, tilting the pan to coat the sides. Add the eggs to the wok and cook, stirring, until thickened, 3 to 4 minutes. Shred or break up the scrambled eggs and set aside.

3. In the same wok, heat 3 tablespoons of the oil over medium-high heat. Add the mango, carrots, onions, peas, corn, and garlic and cook, stirring frequently, until the onions become translucent, 5 to 7 minutes.

4. Stir in the cooked rice, scallions, fish sauce, soy sauce, lime juice, salt, and pepper to taste and the remaining 1 tablespoon of the oil. Cook, stirring, until the rice begins to brown, 5 to 6 minutes. Stir in the cooked eggs and serve.

Pineapple Fried Rice

I love making this rice dish. The pineapple chunks give it an amazing texture, and the sweetness adds a wonderful layer to the overall flavor. Add tofu or chicken for a heartier rice.

MAKES
4 SERVINGS

● DAIRY-FREE
■ VEGETARIAN

1½ cups jasmine rice

5 tablespoons vegetable oil

3 large eggs, beaten

2 cups canned pineapple chunks, drained and chopped (one 20-ounce can; use pineapple packed in juice, *not* syrup)

1 cup diced carrots

1 cup diced yellow onion

1 cup frozen green peas, thawed

1 cup frozen yellow corn kernels, thawed

2 tablespoons minced garlic

½ cup finely chopped scallions

3 tablespoons fish sauce

2 tablespoons gluten-free soy sauce

Salt and freshly ground black pepper

1. Cook the rice according to the package instructions. Allow to cool for at least 2 hours before making the fried rice. (You should have 3 cups of cooked rice.)

2. In a large wok or skillet, heat 1 tablespoon of the oil over medium heat, tilting the pan to coat the sides. Add the eggs to the wok and cook, stirring, until thickened, 3 to 4 minutes. Shred or break up the scrambled eggs and set aside.

3. In the same wok, heat 3 tablespoons of the oil over medium-high heat. Add the pineapple, carrots, onions, peas, corn, and garlic and cook, stirring frequently, until the onions become translucent, 5 to 7 minutes.

4. Stir in the cooked rice, scallions, fish sauce, soy sauce, the remaining 1 tablespoon of the oil, and salt and pepper to taste. Cook, stirring, until the rice begins to brown, 5 to 6 minutes. Stir in the cooked eggs and serve.

Spicy Chicken Chow Fun

This recipe comes from the kitchen of Chef Katie Chin. Chow fun is a wonderful dish that you can get at most Chinese restaurants. It is naturally gluten-free because it uses rice noodles. This is a very spicy dish; use half the amount of chili paste for a more subtle heat.

MAKES
4 SERVINGS

● DAIRY-FREE

FOR THE SAUCE

¼ cup gluten-free soy sauce

¼ cup rice vinegar

¼ cup sugar

¼ cup water

2 teaspoons oyster sauce

FOR THE NOODLES

28 ounces chow fun rice noodles (wide noodles sold fresh in 16-ounce to 32-ounce packages at most Asian markets)

2 teaspoons vegetable oil

2 teaspoons minced garlic

2 teaspoons Thai Kitchen roasted red chili paste

8 ounces ground chicken, cooked

¼ cup minced scallions

¼ cup shredded black fungus mushrooms or dried shiitake mushrooms

1 tablespoon sesame oil

Minced scallions, for garnish

FOR THE SAUCE

1. In a small saucepan, whisk together the soy sauce, vinegar, sugar, water, and oyster sauce. Warm over low heat for 4 to 5 minutes. Remove from heat and set aside.

FOR THE NOODLES

1. Separate the chow fun noodles and cover with plastic wrap until ready to use.

2. Heat a large wok or skillet over medium-high heat and add the vegetable oil. Add the garlic and chili paste and cook, stirring, for about 10 seconds. Add the chicken and cook, stirring, for 3 to 4 minutes. Add in the scallions and mushrooms and stir-fry briefly.

3. Drop the separated noodles, a handful at a time, into the wok while stirring. Continue cooking until the noodles have absorbed all the flavors and are hot. Add the sesame oil and toss.

4. Pour the sauce over the noodles, stir, and serve. Garnish with additional scallions.

▥ VEGETARIAN OPTION

Replace chicken with chopped extra-firm tofu.

Pad Thai

This recipe comes from the kitchen of Chef Katie Chin. Sweet, sour, and salty tastes all blend and balance in this traditional Thai favorite. The fruity-sourness of tamarind is almost impossible to duplicate; the juice is worth searching for in Asian or Indian markets.

MAKES
4 SERVINGS

● DAIRY-FREE

One 14-ounce package rice noodles

¼ cup tamarind juice

1½ tablespoons Thai Kitchen premium fish sauce

1 tablespoon rice vinegar

1 tablespoon sugar

½ teaspoon paprika

2 tablespoons vegetable oil

1 tablespoon minced garlic

16 medium shrimp, peeled and deveined

2 ounces firm tofu, cubed

1 large egg, lightly beaten

½ cup bean sprouts

¼ cup unsalted peanuts, crushed

Sprigs of fresh cilantro, for garnish

Lime, for garnish

1. In a large bowl, soak the rice noodles in cold water for at least 1 hour, or up to overnight. Drain and set aside.

2. In a small bowl, combine the tamarind juice, fish sauce, vinegar, sugar, and paprika.

3. In a large wok or skillet, heat the oil over medium heat and add the garlic. Cook, stirring frequently, until fragrant, about 30 seconds. Add the shrimp, tofu, and egg and cook, stirring, until the egg is scrambled, about 1 to 2 minutes. Add the rice noodles and tamarind juice mixture. Cook, stirring, until everything is combined and well cooked, 1 to 2 minutes.

4. Serve the noodles with bean sprouts on the side, peanuts sprinkled over the top, and with the cilantro and lime-wedge garnishes.

Peanut Noodles

Sweet peanut butter, creamy coconut milk, and strong spices are blended in this easy-to-make favorite. For a more substantial meal, add grilled chicken, tofu, or your favorite vegetables.

MAKES
4 SERVINGS

● DAIRY-FREE

One 14-ounce package rice noodles

2 tablespoons vegetable oil

½ cup peanut butter

2 tablespoons red curry paste

1 cup coconut milk

3 tablespoons fish sauce

2 tablespoons water

2 teaspoons curry powder

1 teaspoon cumin

1 teaspoon salt

1 teaspoon freshly ground black pepper

1. Cook the rice noodles according to the package instructions. Drain and set aside.

2. Meanwhile, in a medium saucepan, heat the oil over medium heat. Add the peanut butter and curry paste and cook, stirring frequently, until the peanut butter is melted and the curry paste is fully incorporated. Stir in the coconut milk and fish sauce and bring to a slow boil. Reduce the heat to medium, cover, and simmer for 8 to 10 minutes. Add in the water, curry powder, cumin, salt, and pepper and simmer, stirring frequently, for 3 to 4 minutes.

3. Pour the sauce over the noodles, mix together, and serve.

Rice Noodles with Black Bean Sauce and Tofu

A simple and elegant tofu dish, perfect for a quick dinner.

MAKES
4 SERVINGS

● DAIRY-FREE

▧ VEGETARIAN

One 14-ounce package rice
noodles

One 14-ounce package extra-
firm tofu

2 cups vegetable stock

½ cup canned fermented
black beans, drained

2 tablespoons rice wine

1 tablespoon minced garlic

1 teaspoon sugar

2 tablespoons gluten-free soy
sauce

1 teaspoon cornstarch

1. Preheat the oven to 350°F.

2. Cook the rice noodles according to the package instructions. Drain and set aside.

3. Slice the tofu lengthwise into quarters. Pat the tofu dry with a paper towel, place in a glass baking dish, and set aside.

4. In a small saucepan, combine the stock, black beans, wine, garlic, and sugar and bring to a boil, stirring occasionally. In a separate small bowl, combine the soy sauce and cornstarch. Mix well and pour slowly into the black bean mixture. Cook, stirring frequently, over medium-high heat until the sauce has thickened.

5. Pour 1 tablespoon of the sauce over each slice of tofu. Place the tofu in the oven and bake for 15 minutes.

6. Pour the remaining sauce over the noodles and toss well. Put a heaping spoonful of noodles on each of the 4 plates. Top each serving with a slice of baked tofu.

SUSHI

Sushi is one of my favorite foods. It is light, delicious, and one of the most creative things you can prepare. Many people think sushi is too difficult to make in the home, but really, it takes no more time than making taco salad! The basic ingredients you will need are seaweed wrappers and rice. Both are naturally gluten-free, and you can find them in most grocery stores. You will also need basic sushi-making equipment; buy a sushi-making kit at an Asian market or from an online store.

Nori (Seaweed)

Dried seaweed is the most important ingredient for sushi making because it is used to wrap up or roll the sushi rice and ingredients.

Sushi Rice Preparation

Japanese sushi rice gets very sticky when it is cooked. You'll appreciate the stickiness as you start making your sushi rolls. You want the rice to stick together well and to bind with the seaweed and ingredients you fill the roll with. Follow this recipe to ensure that your rice has the perfect degree of stickiness.

Sushi Rice

MAKES 4 CUPS

- DAIRY-FREE
- VEGETARIAN

3 cups Japanese-style (short grain) rice

4 cups water

¼ cup rice wine vinegar

1. Wash the rice at least two or three times before beginning the cooking process. You will know the rice is clean if you can pour water on it and it remains clear. After thoroughly washing the rice, combine the rice and water in a saucepan or rice cooker and simmer until the liquid is absorbed, about 20 to 25 minutes. Once the rice is cooked, move it to a bowl and pour the vinegar over it. Mix well and allow the rice to cool.

Dipping Items

Pickled ginger: Typically served on the plate with sushi, pickled ginger is used to cleanse the palate in between bites of sushi.

Soy sauce: Soy sauce is typically made with wheat, but gluten-free varieties are available. See Asian Ingredients to Keep in Your Kitchen (page 98) for recommendations. Soy sauce has a salty flavor that adds a fantastic depth to each bite of sushi.

Wasabi: Wasabi is a green horseradish powder and is turned into wasabi paste by adding water. It is typically added directly to sushi or mixed with soy sauce to create a paste.

Now let's make the sushi!

Types of Sushi

Below are three variations of sushi rolls, followed by some of my favorite ingredient combinations that can be rolled inside.

Maki sushi is my favorite to make, especially when I am putting a bunch of different types of fish and other fixings together. Maki rolls are made by pressing prepared rice onto a sheet of seaweed and placing a variety of fish, vegetables, and fruits inside and then rolling it up and slicing it into bite-sized pieces.

To make maki sushi, start by laying out a sheet of seaweed. Press a thin layer of sushi rice flat onto the seaweed. Next, layer your ingredients of choice on top of the rice and firmly roll it up into a log shape. Slice the log into approximately six even pieces.

Nigiri sushi is a small rectangular piece of rice that is usually topped with fish. Sometimes you will see a small piece of seaweed wrapped around the fish and rice to hold it together. I also like to put a small amount of wasabi between the fish and the rice to ensure I get wasabi in every bite.

To make nigiri sushi, you'll want to start by molding a small fistful of sushi rice into a square shape. Smear a fingertip portion of wasabi on the rice and then lay your favorite type of raw fish on top. Serve with soy sauce.

Temaki sushi are hand rolls that look like ice cream cones. The wrapper is the same seaweed, but instead of rolling the ingredients inside and cutting bite-sized pieces, you just roll the rice and fillings inside the seaweed to look like a cone.

To make a temaki hand roll, start with one piece of seaweed. Press a thin layer of rice flat onto the seaweed. Next layer your ingredients of choice on top of the rice and roll the bundle into a cone shape.

Here are some of my personal favorite rolls! You can use any of these combinations to create either a maki or temaki roll.

NOTE: Always use fresh crabmeat. Imitation crab is made from wheat.

Alaska Roll—salmon, cucumber, asparagus

Asparagus Roll—asparagus

Avocado Roll—avocado

Boston Roll—crabmeat, cucumber

California Roll—crabmeat, avocado

Caterpillar Roll—eel, cucumber, avocado

Citrus Salmon—salmon, mango marinated in lime juice, cucumber, pickled ginger

Crunchy Roll—shrimp tempura, avocado, spicy mayonnaise, cucumber

Cucumber Roll—cucumber

Island Roll—shrimp tempura, crabmeat, mango, avocado, cucumber

Mango Mantra Roll—tuna, mango, spicy mayonnaise, cucumber

Monkey Madness Roll—yellowtail, salmon, eel, cucumber

New York Roll—shrimp, avocado

Philadelphia Roll—smoked salmon, cream cheese, scallions

Pretty'n Pink Roll—tuna, salmon, avocado, spicy mayonnaise

Rainbow Roll—California roll, each slice topped with tuna, salmon, eel, or shrimp

Rock'n'Roll—eel, avocado, spicy mayonnaise

Salmon Roll—salmon

Scallop Roll—scallop

Spicy Salmon Roll—salmon, spicy mayonnaise, scallions, and cucumber

Spicy Scallop Roll—scallop, spicy mayonnaise, scallions, cucumber

Spicy Tuna Roll—tuna, spicy mayonnaise

Spicy Tuna Tempura Roll—tuna tempura, spicy mayonnaise

Spicy Yellowtail Roll—yellowtail, scallions, cucumber

Tempura Shrimp Roll—shrimp tempura, cucumber, avocado, lettuce

Tuna and Avocado Roll—tuna, avocado

Tuna Roll—tuna

Unagi Roll—eel, avocado, cucumber

Yellowtail and Scallion Roll—yellowtail, scallions

MAIN DISHES

The beautiful thing about Asian main dishes is that they are so easy to make and can be cooked in very little time. They also use very few pots and pans, which makes cleaning the kitchen a simple task! The flavors in these recipes are complex; yet they are made with the simplest of ingredients. For example, the first recipe uses a peanut sauce. The base is peanut butter flavored with a variety of Asian spices. Mix and match the sauces, vegetables, and proteins to create an endless array of gluten-free meal options.

Chicken and Broccoli in Peanut Sauce

This spicy dish is so good it should be on the menu of every Asian restaurant. The sauce is so thick and creamy that you'll keep going back for more.

MAKES
4 SERVINGS

● DAIRY-FREE

2 cups white or brown rice

4 tablespoons vegetable oil

½ cup peanut butter

2 tablespoons red curry paste

1 cup coconut milk

3 tablespoons fish sauce

2 tablespoons water

2 teaspoons curry powder

1 teaspoon cumin

1 teaspoon salt

1 teaspoon freshly ground black pepper

3 (about 1 pound) thinly sliced chicken breasts

1 pound broccoli

1. Cook the rice according to the package instructions.

2. Meanwhile, in a medium saucepan, heat 2 tablespoons of the oil over medium heat. Add in the peanut butter and curry paste and cook, stirring frequently, until the peanut butter is melted and the ingredients are well combined, 3 to 4 minutes. Stir in the coconut milk and fish sauce and bring to a slow boil. Reduce the heat, cover, and simmer for 5 to 7 minutes. Add the water, curry powder, cumin, salt, and pepper and simmer, stirring constantly, until the mixture is thickened, 3 to 4 minutes.

3. Dice the chicken and broccoli into small bite sized pieces. In a large skillet, heat the remaining 2 tablespoons of oil over medium-high heat. Add the chicken and cook, stirring frequently, until it begins to brown, 5 to 6 minutes. Add the broccoli and cook, stirring frequently, for 3 to 4 minutes.

4. Pour the peanut sauce over the chicken and broccoli and stir together well. Serve over the rice.

Grilled Tofu and Asparagus with Wasabi Mashed Potatoes

Mashed potatoes are so great spiced up with wasabi. Add a little or a lot of the horseradish depending on how spicy you want your potatoes. If you eat meat, replace the tofu with steak or grilled chicken.

MAKES
4 SERVINGS

■ VEGETARIAN

FOR THE POTATOES

8 russet potatoes

¾ cup skim milk

¼ cup sour cream

1 tablespoon store-bought wasabi

Salt and freshly ground black pepper

FOR THE TOFU AND ASPARAGUS

One 14-ounce package extra-firm tofu

1 bunch asparagus

2 tablespoons olive oil

FOR THE GLAZE

½ cup gluten-free soy sauce

½ cup honey

1 tablespoon ground ginger

FOR THE POTATOES

1. Bring a large pot of water to a boil. Peel the potatoes if desired, slice them in half, and boil until the potatoes are softened, 20 to 25 minutes. It's much easier to peel potatoes before slicing. Drain and return the potatoes to the pot. Add the milk, sour cream, wasabi, salt, and pepper to taste and mash using a potato masher or a hand-held electric mixer. Keep potatoes warm.

FOR THE TOFU AND ASPARAGUS

1. Preheat the grill or a grill pan.

2. Slice the tofu into 4 equal-sized slices. Wash the asparagus and snap off the tough ends. Coat the tofu and asparagus with the oil.

3. Grill the tofu and asparagus for 3 to 4 minutes on each side. Set aside.

FOR THE GLAZE

1. Combine the soy sauce, honey, and ginger in a small saucepan. Bring to a boil over medium-high heat, then cook until the sauce reaches the desired thickness, 10 to 12 minutes.

2. Pour the sauce over the tofu and asparagus and serve with the mashed potatoes on the side.

Pineapple and Green Curry with Jasmine Rice

Over the years I've learned to love curry, especially with pineapple and rice. The sweetness of the pineapple cuts through the curry flavor, and the rice absorbs the spice. Together the combination is perfect! If you're in the mood for meat, add grilled chicken for protein; to keep the dish vegetarian, you can add tofu.

**MAKES
4 SERVINGS**

- DAIRY-FREE
- VEGETARIAN

2 cups jasmine rice

2 tablespoons vegetable oil

1 tablespoon green curry paste

3 cups chopped pineapple (fresh or canned—drained if canned))

1 yellow onion, diced

1 tablespoon minced garlic

One 14 ounce can coconut milk

1 cup vegetable stock

1 teaspoon cornstarch

1. Prepare the rice according to the package instructions.

2. Meanwhile, in a large skillet, heat the oil over medium heat. Add the curry paste and cook, stirring constantly, until it is melted and fragrant, 1 to 2 minutes. Add the pineapple, onions, and garlic and cook, stirring frequently, until tender, 5 to 7 minutes. Add the coconut milk and bring to a boil.

3. In a small bowl, combine the stock and cornstarch to form a smooth paste. Pour into the boiling curry. Simmer until the sauce reaches the desired thickness, 5 to 6 minutes.

4. Serve the curry over the cooked rice.

Grilled Salmon and Green Curry Risotto

A wonderful salmon dish with hints of green curry in the rice. It is my version of an Asian risotto.

MAKES 4 SERVINGS

● DAIRY-FREE

4 salmon steaks (about 1 pound total)

Salt and freshly ground black pepper

2 tablespoons vegetable oil

1 yellow onion, diced

1 tablespoon minced garlic

2 cups jasmine rice

2 cups loosely packed fresh spinach

2 cups vegetable stock

One 14 ounce can coconut milk

2 tablespoons garlic powder

1 tablespoon green curry paste

1. Preheat the grill or a grill pan. Season the salmon with the salt and pepper and grill for 4 to 5 minutes on each side. Set aside.

2. In a large saucepan, heat the oil over medium-high heat. Add the onions and garlic and cook, stirring frequently, until the onions become translucent, 5 to 7 minutes.

3. Add the rice, spinach, stock, coconut milk, garlic powder, and curry paste and cook, stirring frequently, until most of the liquid is absorbed and the rice is fully cooked, about 15 to 18 minutes. Season with the salt and pepper.

4. Serve the grilled salmon over the rice.

VEGETARIAN OPTION

Substitute mushrooms or tofu for the salmon.

Red Curry Vegetable Rice

The play of red curry with fresh vegetables is irresistible.

MAKES
4 SERVINGS

● DAIRY-FREE

▓ VEGETARIAN

2 tablespoons vegetable oil

1 yellow onion, diced

1 tablespoon minced garlic

3 cups vegetable stock

2 cups jasmine rice

2 cups loosely packed fresh
spinach

2 cups thinly sliced
mushrooms

1 cup diced red bell peppers

1 cup green peas

One 14 ounce can coconut
milk

1 tablespoon red curry paste

2 tablespoons garlic powder

Salt and freshly ground black
pepper

1. In a large saucepan, heat the oil over medium-high heat. Add the onions and garlic and cook, stirring frequently until the onions become translucent, 5 to 7 minutes. Add the stock, rice, spinach, mushrooms, bell peppers, peas, coconut milk, curry paste, and garlic powder. Cook, stirring frequently, until most of the liquid is absorbed and the rice is fully cooked, about 15 to 18 minutes. Season with the salt and pepper to taste.

Stir-Fry with Tofu, Green Beans, and Tomatoes

This recipe comes from the kitchen of Chef Katie Chin. It is a light but satisfying vegetarian dish.

MAKES
4 SERVINGS

● DAIRY-FREE

▪ VEGETARIAN

3 tablespoons vegetable oil

10 ounces tofu, cut into
1 x 1 x ½-inch slices

1 tablespoon oyster sauce

8 ounces fresh green beans,
ends broken off

1 cup sliced onion

1 teaspoon minced garlic

¼ cup vegetable stock

2 tomatoes, diced

1 tablespoon Thai Kitchen
chili sauce

1. Heat a large wok or nonstick skillet over high heat (it is easier to cook tofu in a nonstick pan). Add 2 tablespoons of the oil and then the tofu. Cook the tofu for about 2 minutes, then carefully turn it over and cook until lightly browned on both sides, about 2 minutes more.

2. Add the oyster sauce and gently simmer, making sure the tofu doesn't break into pieces, for about 2 minutes. Remove the tofu and place on a platter.

3. Lower the heat to medium-high. Add the remaining 1 tablespoon of oil, the beans, onions, and garlic and cook, stirring, for 1 minute. Add the stock, cover, and cook for 1 minute more.

4. Uncover and continue to cook, stirring, until all the liquid is absorbed, about 2 minutes. Add the tomatoes and chili sauce and stir until well mixed, about 1 minute. Return the tofu to the pan and gently mix together before serving.

Vegetable and Shrimp Beer-Batter Tempura

Redbridge beer is a fantastic addition to a basic tempura recipe. The sweet sorghum adds great flavor to the batter. You can fry anything you would like. I chose my favorites below, but try other things, too. For example, fry grapes and serve them with peanut sauce. You'll have Asian peanut butter and jelly!

MAKES
4 SERVINGS

● DAIRY-FREE

FOR THE BATTER

Onc 12-ounce bottle
   Redbridge gluten-free beer

½ cup cornstarch

½ cup brown rice flour

1 tablespoon sugar

1 package active dry yeast

FOR FRYING

4 cups vegetable or canola oil,
   for frying

1 sweet potato

1 pound jumbo shrimp,
   peeled and deveined

1 pound shiitake mushrooms

1 bunch asparagus

1 peach

FOR SERVING

Gluten-free soy sauce

White or brown rice, cooked

FOR THE BATTER

1. In a large bowl, combine the beer, cornstarch, flour, sugar, and yeast and whisk together well.

FOR FRYING

1. In a large skillet or pot, heat the oil over medium-high heat; it's ready when you see little bubbles in the oil.

2. Slice everything you are going to fry into bite-sized pieces. Dip the foods into the batter and coat well. Carefully add in batches to the hot oil and fry everything until the batter turns a deep golden brown, about 5 minutes.

3. Serve with soy sauce and white or brown rice.

Soy-Glazed Salmon with Brown Rice and Steamed Vegetables

Delicious sweet-glazed salmon and freshly steamed vegetables nutty with brown rice are the perfect combination.

MAKES 4 SERVINGS

● DAIRY-FREE

½ cup gluten-free soy sauce

½ cup honey

2 tablespoons ground ginger

4 cups water

2 cups brown rice

2 cups chopped fresh spinach

1 cup shiitake mushrooms, sliced

1 yellow onion, finely diced

4 salmon steaks (about 1 pound total)

1. In a small saucepan, combine the soy sauce, honey, and ginger. Simmer over medium heat until a thick sauce forms, 12 to 15 minutes.

2. In a large saucepan, combine the water, rice, spinach, mushrooms, and onions. Bring to a boil, then reduce the heat, cover, and simmer until the liquid is absorbed and the rice is fully cooked, about 20 minutes.

3. Meanwhile, preheat the grill or a grill pan.

4. Pour 1 tablespoon of the soy sauce-honey glaze over each salmon steak and rub it into the fish. Cook the fish for 5 minutes on each side, or until the glaze has caramelized.

5. Put a heaping spoonful of the rice mixture on each plate and pour the remaining glaze over the rice. Top each with a salmon steak.

■ VEGETARIAN OPTION

Substitute tofu for the salmon.

Fried Eggplant with Garlic-Ginger Sauce and Jasmine Rice

MAKES
4 SERVINGS

● DAIRY-FREE

▨ VEGETARIAN

Eggplant is a wonderful ingredient. The soft texture works well with the crispy breading, and the garlic-ginger sauce adds the perfect amount of spice.

FOR THE GARLIC-GINGER SAUCE

1 cup grated carrots

1 cup shiitake mushrooms, sliced thinly

1 cup vegetable stock

½ cup gluten-free soy sauce

¼ cup fish sauce

¼ cup honey

2 tablespoons minced garlic

1 tablespoon chili flakes

1 tablespoon ground ginger

FOR THE RICE AND EGGPLANT

1½ cups jasmine rice

2 large eggs

¼ cup gluten-free soy sauce

½ cup brown rice flour

½ cup cornstarch

½ tablespoon salt

2 large eggplants

3 cups (or enough to submerge the eggplant halfway) vegetable or canola oil, for frying

FOR THE GARLIC-GINGER SAUCE

1. In a large saucepan, combine the carrots, mushrooms, stock, soy sauce, fish sauce, honey, garlic, chili flakes and ginger and cook over medium heat until reduced by half and a thick sauce is formed, about 15 minutes. Set aside.

FOR THE RICE AND EGGPLANT

1. Cook the rice according to the package instructions.

2. In a small bowl, whisk together the eggs and soy sauce. In a separate small bowl, mix together the flour, cornstarch, and salt.

3. Slice the eggplants into 2-inch squares about ½ inch thick. Dip the eggplant into the egg-and-soy-sauce mixture and then coat it with the flour-and-cornstarch mixture.

4. In a large skillet, heat the oil over medium-high heat; it's ready when you see little bubbles forming in the oil. Fry the eggplant until the batter turns golden brown, 4 to 5 minutes per side.

5. Gently stir the fried eggplant into the sauce. Pour heaping portions of the eggplant and sauce over the rice and serve.

Steamed Chicken with Broccoli

A light and fit dish for those days when you're watching what you eat.

● DAIRY-FREE

FOR THE CHICKEN

3 boneless, skinless chicken
   breasts (about 1 pound)

1 head broccoli, chopped

FOR THE SAUCE

1 tablespoon vegetable oil

1 yellow onion, chopped

2 scallions with tops, chopped

1 tablespoon minced garlic

2 cups chicken stock

1 tablespoon cornstarch

1 teaspoon ground ginger

1 teaspoon salt

1 teaspoon sugar

FOR SERVING

White or brown rice, steamed

FOR THE CHICKEN

1. Prepare a steamer basket over a pot of simmering water.

2. Slice the chicken and broccoli into bite-sized pieces; place the chicken in the steamer and fully cook, about 35 minutes. Add broccoli for last 3 to 5 minutes.

FOR THE SAUCE

1. In a medium saucepan, heat the oil over medium-high heat. Add the onions, scallions, and garlic and cook, stirring frequently, until the onions become translucent, 5 to 7 minutes.

2. In a small bowl, combine the stock, cornstarch, ginger, salt, and sugar. Whisk the ingredients together and pour into the saucepan. Cook over medium heat, stirring frequently, until a thick sauce is formed, 4 to 5 minutes.

3. Pour the sauce over the chicken and broccoli and serve with steamed white or brown rice.

VEGETARIAN OPTION

Replace the chicken with tofu and use vegetable stock in place of the chicken stock. Steam for only 10, not 35, minutes.

Chicken with Cashew Nuts

Crunchy cashews and salty soy sauce make a perfect match in this traditional chicken dish. Add in as many vegetables as you can and enjoy them on a bed of warm rice.

MAKES
4 SERVINGS

● DAIRY-FREE

2 cups white or brown rice

2 tablespoons vegetable oil

3 boneless, skinless chicken breasts, cubed (about 1 pound)

2 cups shiitake mushrooms, sliced

1 cup chopped scallions

1 cup shredded carrots

1 cup whole cashews, chopped

1 cup chicken stock

3 tablespoons gluten-free soy sauce

1 tablespoon cornstarch

1 ½ teaspoons garlic powder

1 ½ teaspoons ground ginger

1 teaspoon salt

1. Prepare the rice according to the package instructions.

2. In a large wok or skillet, heat the oil over medium-high heat. Add the chicken and cook, stirring frequently, until almost fully cooked, 8 to 10 minutes. Add the mushrooms, scallions, carrots, and cashews. Cook, stirring frequently, for 3 to 4 minutes.

3. In a small bowl, whisk together the stock, soy sauce, cornstarch, garlic powder, ginger, and salt.

4. Pour the sauce over the chicken and vegetables in the wok and cook, stirring frequently, until the sauce thickens, 5 to 7 minutes.

5. Serve over the rice.

Moo Shu Beef and Vegetables

Classic moo shu pancakes are off-limits in the Gluten-free universe. But don't worry. Just replace them with either fresh lettuce-leaf cups or corn tortillas. It is a simple solution filled with big flavors.

MAKES
4 SERVINGS

● DAIRY-FREE

4 tablespoons vegetable oil

3 large eggs, beaten

1 pound thinly sliced beef steak

2 tablespoons cornstarch

8 ounces shiitake mushrooms, thinly sliced

2 cups shredded carrots

2 cups shredded green cabbage

½ cup chopped scallions

½ cup gluten-free soy sauce

½ cup rice wine

1 tablespoon minced garlic

1 teaspoon ground ginger

Corn tortillas or iceberg lettuce leaves

1. In a large wok or skillet, heat 1 tablespoon of the oil over medium-high heat, tipping the wok to spread the oil evenly. Add the eggs. Allow them to cook undisturbed. They will form a solid "disk" on the bottom of the wok. When the eggs are fully cooked, remove the "disk" and set aside.

2. Slice the steak into long, thin strips. Place it in a large bowl and coat with the cornstarch.

3. Add the remaining 3 tablespoons of the oil to the wok and heat over medium-high heat. Add the beef and cook, stirring frequently, for 2 to 3 minutes.

4. Add the mushrooms, carrots, cabbage, scallions, soy sauce, wine, garlic, and ginger and cook, stirring frequently, until a thick sauce forms around the meat and vegetables, 8 to 10 minutes.

5. Roll up the disk egg and slice it into thin strips. Stir the egg strips into the beef and vegetable mixture and serve wrapped in the tortillas, or use the lettuce leaves as cups, filling each with a heaping spoonful of the mixture.

Steamed Whole Fish with Black Bean Sauce

This recipe comes from the kitchen of Chef Katie Chin. The black beans lend a fantastic texture to this dramatic presentation.

MAKES
4 SERVINGS

● DAIRY-FREE

2 tablespoons salted black beans

1 tablespoon vegetable oil

2 teaspoons fish sauce

1 teaspoon finely chopped fresh ginger

1 teaspoon gluten-free soy sauce

1 teaspoon minced garlic

½ teaspoon salt

¼ teaspoon sesame oil

¼ teaspoon sugar

1½ pounds whole walleyed pike or red snapper, well cleaned

2 scallions with tops

Ice water

1. In a small bowl, cover the black beans with warm water. Stir the beans for about 2 minutes to remove excess salt. Remove the beans from the water, rinse, and drain well. Set aside.

2. In a small bowl, mix together the vegetable oil, fish sauce, ginger, soy sauce, garlic, salt, sesame oil, and sugar. Slash the fish crosswise 3 times on each side. Rub the cavity and outside of the fish with the oil mixture. Spread the black beans evenly over the fish. Cover and refrigerate for 30 minutes or longer.

3. Cut the scallions into 2-inch pieces and shred lengthwise into fine strips. Place in a bowl with ice water to cover and let stand until the strips curl, about 10 minutes.

4. Place the fish on a heatproof plate. Put the plate on a rack in a steamer basket over boiling water, cover, and steam until the fish flakes easily with a fork, about 10 minutes. (Add more boiling water if necessary.) Serve garnished with the scallions.

Mexican
GLUTEN-FREE
COOKING

FROM CHEF
Edgar Steele
of Café Atlantico

Latin cuisine is as beautifully diverse as the many different South and Central American countries it represents. Today we know it both in its traditional state and with added twists, which many have come to love as Nuevo Latino. When focusing on its tradition through a general eye, we find Latin cuisine to be excitingly full and rich yet not heavy in flavors. Onions, garlic, and spices are used to tantalize the palate, which is then blown away with citrus, tropical fruits, and roots integrated into dishes.

Latin cooking and gluten-free diets are intertwined nicely, as several Latin staples—such as yucca and corn flour—can be natural substitutions for otherwise non-friendly glutinous ingredients. In the case of many traditional and "nuevo" dishes alike, farmed vegetables and herbs as well as meats are in the spotlight, and recipes seldom call for anything with gluten. When wheat flour is called for in a recipe, it can easily be replaced with several root-vegetable flours. For a person with Celiac Disease who enjoys authenticity and tradition in its pure form, Latin cuisine is a perfect fit, as it is nearly gluten-free already!

Latin cuisine comprises the foods and beverages of several unique countries, and with each comes a bounty of diverse cultural cooking techniques, ingredients, and flavors. With such a wide range of land and culture represented under one name, the resulting space available for new and exciting dishes, and room for creativity within these parameters is nearly endless. Common-thread ingredients seen throughout many of Latin cuisines include—but are certainly not limited to—corn, plantains, coconut, several varieties of beans, yucca, potatoes, and rice, along with a colorful range of nuts, fruits, meats, and seafood.

The list of ingredients is limited only to your palate's preference, and with so many gluten-free choices, there is certainly something for everyone to love. Vegetable starches and fruit pectin, as opposed to flour, are used as thickeners, while many dishes are centered on fruits and vegetables, prepared simply.

Corn, native to El Salvador, is used as a base to prepare myriad dishes and is available in many different forms. Corn flour is used to prepare a dough, which after delicate handwork and frying becomes a soft yet slightly crunchy crust around a filling of cheese, meat, and beans, flattened into the shape of a pancake. This is the *pupusa*, and many countries including Mexico, Venezuela, Colombia, Guatemala, and the Honduras, offer their own interpretations. Corn flour is also used to prepare sopes, which are small fried corn patties native to Mexico, often stuffed with sausage and potatoes and topped with thickened cream and scallions. Cornmeal made from dried corn kernels, can be used to prepare cornbread and grits. Masa harina is a unique preparation of corn—a powder made from a dough of corn. The kernels are soaked, ground, dried, and then pulverized. This powder is a base with which sauces and soups are thickened and tortillas and tamales are prepared.

In Puerto Rico plantains are cooked in many different ways and are eaten from morning till night. Tostones are fried green plantains in the shape of a flat chip. The plantains are cut into equal-sized pieces and fried. After being fried, they are smashed with a tostonera and fried once more until golden, and served as a side dish or snack with a creamy tomato and garlic sauce.

Another characteristic that gives such appeal to Latin cuisine is the use of tropical fruits in both savory and sweet preparations. Aguas frescas, literally translated as "fresh water," are juices of fruits often mixed with water and sometimes sugar for extra sweetness, especially when using an acidic fruit, and are commonly found in Mexico and the Caribbean. Common fruits from which aguas frescas are prepared include papaya, mango, cucumber, several varieties of melon, and some acidic fruits such as orange, lime, lemon, pineapple, and tamarind. These juices are sometimes blended with other flavors, such as serrano or jalapeño chiles, salt, and spices such as cinnamon, star anise, cloves, or nutmeg.

A fully compiled list of natural-ingredient preparations from Latin America could easily render the largest book ever published, and because of this we take comfort in always finding new things to enjoy. It is easy and exciting to bring past dishes back to life, to rediscover things our ancestors grew to love centuries ago. In an interesting yet natural twist, many dishes we know and love today are reinvented dishes from these traditions. Nuevo-Latino cuisine is exactly that: reinvented dishes that have represented the cultures of Latin America through history.

Café Atlantico is a Nuevo-Latino restaurant. The term is literally translated as "new Latin cuisine." I began working at the café over five years ago, and even then the menu was eighty percent gluten-free. Over time, especially after I discovered the National Foundation for Celiac Awareness, the menu has become very friendly to anyone with dietary preferences and restrictions. What at one point seemed to be a complicated operation—adjusting the menus to meet these needs—has become easier with simple ingredient substitutions. After seeing incredible results and the sincerely happy expressions on the faces of our guests, we have applied these same standards to all the restaurants in our company, ThinkFoodGroup.

Our "ravioli" makes use of thinly sliced fruits and vegetables as wrappers for both sweet and savory creamy fillings. We prepare "pastas" made from the juices of fruits and vegetables, with the aid of a strong jelling agent called agar-agar. Tomatoes, for instance, may be juiced and heated with the agar-agar. Once the boiling point is reached, a thin layer of the liquid is poured onto a flat surface and allowed to cool. Then the jelled tomato is cut into thin strips resembling pasta, which can be tossed with a light sauce and even heated.

For a person with a food restriction or allergy such as Celiac Disease, eating in restaurants can be a difficult and even scary experience. It is crucial that a guest's food requests be directly communicated to the appropriate person, and that person is often the chef. The chef controls everything that comes out of the kitchen and in most cases is the person who knows if a dish is safe for someone to eat based on their situation. At ThinkFoodGroup, our menus identify which dishes contain gluten, seafood, dairy products, nuts, and so on. I have found this to be a great way to help people with their selections, though I still suggest that the person communicate his or her requests directly to the chef. I consider it to be no different from the telephone game: one person begins with a message, and once that message is passed between two or three people, key elements have gone missing.

This communication is important not only because you want to know what you can eat, but because it is easy in many cases for a plate to be made gluten-free in the finishing stages simply by withholding a garnish or another element. For example, our liquid chocolate cake contains gluten, but an equally extravagant dessert can be prepared in a matter of minutes using the other components of that dish: the chocolate flan, lime, marinated bananas, and banana mousse. Another example is the café's guacamole, prepared tableside and served with steamed flour tortillas. Because of the tortillas, the guacamole is designated on the allergy menu as containing gluten. Upon request to the chef however, those tortillas may be replaced with thinly sliced jícama, a root vegetable native to Mexico. The jícama can be used exactly the same way as tortillas are—as scoops for guacamole.

In countless ways Latin cuisine, both traditional and new, can accommodate a gluten-free diet. Knowledge and awareness on the part of both the chef and the diner are crucial to creating safe, optimal dining experiences.

The menus at Café Atlantico may sound quite complicated to most home cooks, but don't be scared off too easily. The recipes ahead are adapted so any home cook can master the techniques.

Buen provecho!

MEXICAN INGREDIENTS *to Keep in Your Kitchen*

Mexican cooking is all about the spice and zing! Most of the dishes you'll find in this section use a combination of the same spices—chili powder, cumin, garlic, and paprika, so it's easy to always have them on hand. The other great thing about Mexican cooking is that it is mainly based on corn, which makes it a perfect cuisine for a gluten-free diet. Corn tortillas are used for tacos, enchiladas, and taquitos while masa (corn flour) is used to make tamales and empanadas. With nearly no substitutions necessary, you've got a delicious gluten-free Mexican meal.

SPICES

I always purchase McCormick spices (www.mccormick.com). It is a company policy to always declare on the label if any one of twelve allergens is used in their products, including wheat. If there is no declaration on the package, the only ingredient in the container is the pure spice.

- Chili flakes
- Chili powder
- Cumin
- Garlic powder
- Paprika

RICE AND QUINOA

I generally always buy Thai Kitchen (www.thaikitchen.com), Lundberg (www.lundberg.com), or Bob's Red Mill (www.bobsredmill.com) brand products. These companies certify their products as gluten-free and produced in facilities that are free of contamination.

- Brown rice
- Jasmine rice
- Quinoa
- White rice

OTHER INGREDIENTS

Most essential Mexican ingredients can be found in your regular grocery story. You'll see below that none of these ingredients is considered a "specialty item"; rather they are normal foods that we eat every day. With just a little guidance and some Mexican spices, they can be cooked into a marvelous Mexican feast.

- Avocados
- Chicken stock (Swanson's is gluten-free)
- Cilantro
- Coconut milk
- Corn tortillas
- Garlic
- Ground beef, turkey, chicken, or seafood
- Lime juice
- Mangoes
- Masa
- Peaches
- Plantains
- Red onions
- Tomatoes

STARTERS AND SALSAS

The first course of a Mexican meal is usually my favorite largely because it is usually so delicious that it leaves my palate craving the next course. I love a combination of light and rich flavors in each starter, and I love finding ways to incorporate the first part of the meal throughout the rest. For example, I like to use a salsa as a topping or sauce on a piece of grilled fish. The flavor combinations are delightful and can be tweaked by using many different preparation methods to create hundreds of different dishes.

Guacamole

Guacamole is the ultimate party food, and this recipe has just the right amount of flair! Be sure to use soft avocados. The test? Press gently on the skin; if there is a slight give, you've got the perfect avocado.

MAKES
4 SERVINGS

● DAIRY-FREE

▦ VEGETARIAN

4 large ripe avocados

3 tablespoons fresh lime juice

1 red onion, diced

1 cup finely chopped fresh cilantro

1 garlic clove, minced

1 tablespoon diced serrano chile (seeds removed)

1 large tomato, diced

Corn chips, for serving

1. Cut the avocados in half and remove the pit from each. Scoop out the flesh and put it into a large bowl. Add the lime juice and mash with a fork.

2. Add the onions, cilantro, garlic, and chile and mix together well. Gently fold in the tomatoes and serve with the corn chips.

Mango, Tuna, and Avocado Ceviche with Crunchy Corn Nuts

The first time I tried ceviche was at Café Atlantico. Chef Edgar Steele kept telling me it was one of the most amazing things I would ever taste. I was skeptical, but finally gave in and tasted Café Atlantico's tuna avocado ceviche. This is my interpretation of the same dish with an added tropical flourish.

MAKES
4 SERVINGS

● DAIRY-FREE

1 pound sushi-grade
   yellowfin tuna,
   chopped finely into cubes

1 cup cubed mango

½ cup finely chopped fresh
   cilantro

½ cup finely diced red onion

¼ cup lime juice

½ teaspoon salt

1 ripe avocado

1 cup corn nuts, crushed

1. In a large bowl, combine the tuna, mango, cilantro, onions, lime juice, and salt, stirring gently. Spoon the mixture onto a serving plate.

2. Cut the avocado in half and remove the pit. Slice the avocado and lay slices over the tuna mixture. Sprinkle the corn nuts generously on top. Serve immediately or chill until ready to serve.

Tuna Tartar

This is a simple and elegant dish for a summer day. Be sure to use only tuna from a trusted market and keep it cold. It pairs really well with a cool glass of white wine.

MAKES
4 SERVINGS

● DAIRY-FREE

1 pound sushi-grade
yellowfin tuna,
chopped finely into cubes

1 cup diced red onion

1 cup finely chopped fresh
chives

2 tablespoons extra-virgin
olive oil

2 tablespoons fresh lemon
juice

Salt and freshly ground black
pepper

1. In a medium bowl, combine the tuna, onions, chives, oil, and lemon juice. Stir together gently. Season with the salt and pepper. Serve immediately or chill until ready to serve.

Chihuahua Cheese Dip

Chihuahua cheese is not easy to find, but if you can find a specialty cheese shop that sells this creamy cheese, you'll never buy any other kind ever again! If you can't find it, use cheddar or Monterey Jack. You'll still have an amazing dip.

MAKES
8 SERVINGS

■ VEGETARIAN

One 12-ounce bottle
Redbridge gluten-free beer

1 pound Chihuahua cheese,
cut into small cubes (see
Headnote)

½ to 1 teaspoon chili flakes
(depending on how spicy
you want it)

Bite-sized vegetables, rice
crackers, and gluten-free
pretzels, for dipping

1. In a large saucepan, heat the beer over medium heat. Once it comes to a slow boil, add the cheese, stirring constantly until the cheese is melted and the mixture is smooth. Add the chili flakes and cook, stirring constantly, 1 minute more.

2. Remove the cheese mixture from the heat and place in a fondue pot. Keep warm on the low heat setting (or over a tea light, depending on the type of fondue pot). Serve with the vegetables, rice crackers, and pretzels.

Corn Tortilla Soup

This recipe comes from the kitchen of Chef Edgar Steele of Café Atlantico.
It is a heart-warming start to a Nuevo-Latino meal.

MAKES
4 SERVINGS

VEGETARIAN

1 tablespoon butter

1 cup diced yellow onion

2 teaspoons diced serrano
chile

1 dried bay leaf

4 cups fresh corn kernels

2 cups water

¼ cup heavy cream

8 sprigs of fresh cilantro

2½ cups crushed corn tortilla
chips

Salt

1 cup strained Greek yogurt
or tzatziki

1. In a large saucepan, melt the butter over low heat. Add the onions, chile, and bay leaf and cook, stirring, until the onions are softened and translucent, about 15 minutes. Add the corn, water, and heavy cream and bring to a simmer, allowing to cook for 20 minutes, stirring occasionally.

2. Add the cilantro and 2 cups of the tortilla chips and cook until the chips are softened, about 5 minutes more. Remove from the heat and remove bay leaf.

3. In a food processor, blend the mixture in batches on high speed until smooth. Be careful when you're blending, as the contents are extremely hot. Adjust the consistency of the soup with more water, if needed.

4. Add salt to taste and serve the soup hot, garnished with the yogurt and the remaining tortilla chips.

Jícama-Avocado Salad with Citrus Vinaigrette

This recipe comes from the kitchen of Chef Edgar Steele of Café Atlantico. Jícama is an amazing vegetable that is light, crisp, and fresh. The salad has a strong citrus flavor that is perfectly offset by the saltiness of the corn nuts and the boldness of the Dijon mustard.

MAKES
4 SERVINGS

● DAIRY-FREE

■ VEGETARIAN

FOR THE CITRUS VINAIGRETTE

¼ cup fresh orange juice

2 tablespoons fresh lemon juice

2 tablespoons fresh lime juice

2 teaspoons Dijon mustard

½ cup canola oil

Salt

FOR THE JÍCAMA SALAD

2 cups peeled and diced jícama

½ cup diced red onion

½ cup fresh white corn kernels, blanched in simmering water for a minute and cooled

Grated zest of ½ lemon

FOR THE CITRUS VINAIGRETTE

1. In a small bowl, mix together the juices and mustard. While briskly whisking, slowly add the canola oil until a homogenous mixture is achieved. Add salt to taste.

FOR THE JÍCAMA SALAD

1. In a separate bowl, mix together the jícama, onions, corn, and lemon zest. Add the citrus vinaigrette and toss to coat.

2. Place the avocado halves, cut side down, on a cutting board. Cut lengthwise into ⅛-inch thick slices, making sure to keep the original shape of the avocado as you cut. Press down and away lightly on the cut avocado to fan the slices out like a hand of cards. Do the same with the remaining avocado halves. (To prevent the fruit from browning while you work, place a small piece of plastic wrap directly on the surface of the avocado.)

3. Place a large spoonful of the jícama salad in the center of a plate. Being careful not to disrupt the shape of your beautifully cut avocado, place one fanned half on top of the jícama salad.

2 ripe avocados, peeled, halved, and pitted

2 teaspoons extra-virgin olive oil, for drizzling

2 tablespoons chopped fresh chives, for garnish

¼ cup corn nuts, crushed to a powder, for garnish

Sprigs of fresh cilantro, for garnish

Sea salt

4. Drizzle a bit of olive oil over the avocado and sprinkle the chives and corn nuts on top. Drizzle a bit of the citrus vinaigrette around the plate and garnish with the cilantro. Sprinkle some sea salt over the entire plate and serve.

Watermelon and Halloumi Cheese Salad with a Citrus-Mint Dressing

The watermelon is sweet and has a "pop" when you bite into it. Halloumi cheese, from Cyprus, is a mix of goat's and sheep's milk. It is salty and has a firm texture. The contrasting flavors, with the lime juice and mint, make for a perfect summer salad.

**MAKES
6 SERVINGS**

VEGETARIAN

8 ounces halloumi cheese, cut into bite-sized chunks

2 pounds seedless watermelon, cut into small chunks

¼ cup lime juice

1 cup fresh mint leaves, finely chopped

1. In a large bowl, gently stir together the cheese and watermelon. In a small bowl, whisk together the lime juice and mint leaves and pour over the watermelon and cheese. Refrigerate for about 1 hour before serving to allow the flavors to meld together.

● **DAIRY-FREE OPTION**

Use your favorite soy-based cheese in place of the halloumi.

Fried Plantains
with Peach Chutney

This sweet and savory starter comes from the kitchen of Chef Edgar Steele of Café Atlantico. I like to leave the skin on the peaches, but if you don't like the texture, peel the peaches before using. If you can't find crème fraîche in your local supermarket, substitute sour cream.

MAKES
4 SERVINGS

■ VEGETARIAN

FOR THE PEACH CHUTNEY

1 tablespoon butter

2 tablespoons diced red onion

1 tablespoon chopped fresh
   ginger

½ fresh bay leaf

¼ cinnamon stick

3 ripe peaches, diced

1 tablespoon extra-virgin
   olive oil

2 teaspoons fresh lime juice

2 teaspoons honey

Salt and freshly ground black
   pepper

FOR THE PLANTAINS

4 cups vegetable oil, for frying

3 semi-ripe plantains
   (yellow with some brown
   and black spots)

3 tablespoons sugar

Salt

¼ cup crème fraîche

FOR THE PEACH CHUTNEY

1. In a small saucepan, heat the butter over medium-low heat. Add the onions, ginger, bay leaf, and cinnamon stick and cook, stirring, until the onions become translucent and slightly caramel in color, about 20 minutes. Add the peaches, olive oil, lime juice, and honey and allow to simmer until the peaches are very soft, about 15 minutes. Remove the bay leaf and add salt and pepper to taste.

FOR THE PLANTAINS

1. In a large saucepan, heat the vegetable oil over medium-high heat until it reaches 350°F.

2. Peel the plantains and cut them into slices lengthwise about 1 ½ inches thick. Carefully place the plantains in the oil and fry until golden on the outside, 2 to 4 minutes. Transfer the plantains to paper towels to absorb the excess oil. Season with the sugar and with salt to taste.

3. To serve, top the hot plantains with the peach chutney and some dollops of the crème fraîche.

Mango-Avocado Salsa

The flavors of the mango go perfectly with tomatoes, onions, and cilantro.
This salsa works perfectly on corn chips, on chicken or fish, or pureed into
a marinade for grilling.

MAKES
6 SERVINGS

● DAIRY-FREE

▩ VEGETARIAN

1 large ripe mango, diced

1 large tomato, diced

1 ripe avocado, peeled, pitted,
and diced

1 red onion, diced

1 to 2 cups finely chopped
fresh cilantro

1 garlic clove, minced

¼ cup lime juice

Corn chips, for serving

1. In a medium bowl, combine the mango, tomatoes, avocado, onions, cilantro, garlic, and lime juice. Serve with the corn chips.

Pico de Gallo

A simple standby that works wonderfully with any Latin dish!

MAKES
6 SERVINGS

● DAIRY-FREE

▪ VEGETARIAN

6 large tomatoes, diced

1 medium yellow onion, diced

½ cup chopped fresh cilantro

1 small serrano chile, seeded
and finely diced (adjust
amount based on how spicy
you want the salsa to be)

¼ cup fresh lime juice

1 teaspoon garlic powder

Salt and freshly ground black
pepper

Corn chips, for serving

1. In a large bowl, combine the tomatoes, onions, cilantro, chile, lime juice, and garlic powder. Add salt and pepper to taste. Serve with the corn chips.

Fresh Peach Salsa

All of my friends ask for this salsa when they come over. The flavors of the peach marry magically with the tomato, onion, and cilantro. I like to use a combination of white and yellow peaches to bring more color into the salsa. I also like to leave the skin on the peaches, but if you don't like the texture, peel the peaches before you chop them.

**MAKES
6 SERVINGS**

● DAIRY-FREE

■ VEGETARIAN

2 cups chopped fresh peaches

¼ cup chopped red onion

3 tablespoons lime juice

2 tablespoons finely chopped jalapeño chile (seeds removed)

1 garlic clove, minced

1 tablespoon chopped fresh cilantro

Corn chips, for serving

1. In a medium bowl, stir together the peaches, onions, lime juice, chile, garlic, and cilantro. Serve immediately with corn chips or chill until ready to serve.

STAPLES AND MAIN DISHES

The main dishes of the Mexican section start off with very basic preparations and gradually get more advanced. My favorite part about this section is that in every single recipe, the ingredients are naturally gluten-free and require no conversions. Mexican cuisine in general is heavily based around rice and corn, making these recipes naturally and deliciously gluten-free. They use corn tortillas, masa (cornmeal), fresh meats, fruits, vegetables, and spices.

Each dish starts with a basic recipe, but use a little bit of creativity to alter combinations and make them your own! Use your favorite proteins and vegetables.

Note: Every recipe can easily be converted to vegetarian by simply forgoing the meat or seafood. Replace meat items with more vegetables or tofu. For dairy-free substitutions, use finely grated soy cheese in place of other cheeses.

Enchiladas: Cheese, Beef, Chicken, Seafood, or Vegetable

Enchiladas are a staple of traditional Mexican restaurants in the United States. The basic ingredients are simply corn tortillas, cheese, and enchilada sauce. To be more creative, follow the recipes for beef, chicken, seafood, and vegetable enchiladas—or try a combination!

MAKES 12 ENCHILADAS

FOR THE CHEESE ENCHILADAS

2 cups canned tomato sauce

2 cups water

2 tablespoons chili powder

1 tablespoon garlic powder

1 tablespoon ground cumin

1 tablespoon onion powder

2 tablespoons cornstarch

12 corn tortillas

8 ounces grated cheese, plus extra for topping (a cheddar–Monterey Jack blend is best)

Guacamole (page 151) and sour cream, for serving

Cheese Enchiladas

1. Preheat the oven to 350°F.

2. In a medium saucepan, combine the tomato sauce, water, chili powder, garlic powder, onion powder, and cumin and cook over medium-high heat, stirring constantly, until the mixture comes to a boil. Reduce the heat to medium and allow to simmer for about 5 minutes.

3. In a small bowl, mix the cornstarch with 1 to 2 tablespoons of water to make a paste. Stir the paste into the sauce and cook until the mixture thickens. Remove from the heat.

4. Cover the bottom of a 9 x 13-inch casserole dish with a thin layer of the sauce.

5. Fill each tortilla with a handful of the cheese and roll up. Layer the rolled tortillas in the casserole dish and top with the remaining sauce. Sprinkle additional cheese on top of the tortilla rolls and bake for 25 minutes.

6. Serve hot with the guacamole and sour cream.

2 tablespoons olive oil

1 cup diced yellow onion

1 garlic clove, minced

1 pound ground beef

1 tablespoon chili powder

1 tablespoon ground cumin

1 tablespoon paprika

1 teaspoon salt

1 to 2 cups water

Beef Enchiladas

1. In a large sauté pan, heat the oil over medium-high heat. Add the onions and garlic and cook, stirring frequently, until lightly browned, 5 to 7 minutes. Add the beef, chili powder, cumin, paprika, and salt; mix together well, and cook 1 to 2 minutes. Add the water (just enough to cover the meat) and cook, stirring constantly, until the beef is fully cooked, no pink spots remaining, 10 to 12 minutes.

2. Proceed as in steps 4–6 of the cheese enchilada recipe, page 164, using this filling in place of the cheese.

FOR THE CHICKEN
ENCHILADAS

2 tablespoons olive oil

1 cup diced yellow onion

1 garlic clove, minced

3 boneless, skinless chicken breasts, cubed (about 1 pound)

1 tablespoon chili powder

1 tablespoon ground cumin

1 tablespoon paprika

1 teaspoon salt

½ cup water

Chicken Enchiladas

1. In a large sauté pan, heat the oil over medium-high heat. Add the onions and garlic and cook, stirring frequently, until lightly browned, 5 to 7 minutes. Add the chicken, chili powder, cumin, paprika, and salt and mix together well. Add the water and cook, stirring frequently, until the chicken is fully cooked, 10 to 12 minutes.

2. Proceed as in steps 4–6 of the cheese enchilada recipe, page 164, using this filling in place of the cheese.

CONTINUES

Seafood Enchiladas

FOR THE SEAFOOD ENCHILADAS

3 tablespoons olive oil

1 cup diced yellow onion

1 garlic clove, minced

½ pound medium shrimp, peeled, deveined, and chopped into small pieces

½ pound sea or bay scallops, chopped into small pieces

1 tablespoon chili powder

1 tablespoon ground cumin

1 tablespoon paprika

1 teaspoon salt

1. In a large sauté pan, heat the oil over medium-high heat. Add the onions and garlic and cook, stirring frequently, until lightly browned, 5 to 7 minutes. Add the shrimp, scallops, chili powder, cumin, paprika, and salt and cook, stirring frequently, until the shrimp turn pink and the scallops have a sear, 4 to 5 minutes.

2. Proceed as in steps 4–6 of the cheese enchilada recipe, page 164, using this filling in place of the cheese.

Vegetable Enchiladas

FOR THE VEGETABLE ENCHILADAS

3 tablespoons olive oil

1 cup diced yellow onion

1 garlic clove, minced

2 green bell peppers, sliced

2 red bell peppers, sliced

1 zucchini, chopped

1 yellow squash, chopped

1 tablespoon chili powder

1 tablespoon ground cumin

1 tablespoon paprika

1 teaspoon salt

1. In a large sauté pan, heat the oil over medium-high heat. Add the onions and garlic and cook, stirring frequently, until lightly browned, 5 to 7 minutes. Add the bell peppers, zucchini, squash, chili powder, cumin, paprika, and salt and cook, stirring frequently, until vegetables are tender, about 5 minutes.

2. Proceed as in steps 4–6 of the cheese enchilada recipe, page 164, using this filling in place of the cheese.

Chicken Fajitas

Fajitas are easier to make than you might think. I always used to be intrigued at restaurants when my fajitas would come out of the kitchen still sizzling on the plate. I thought the cast-iron plate made all the difference! With this recipe, you can make fajitas that are just as good as any restaurant's, right in your own kitchen.

MAKES
4 SERVINGS

4 boneless, skinless chicken breasts (about 1½ pounds total)

1 green bell pepper

1 orange bell pepper

1 red bell pepper

1 yellow bell pepper

1 yellow onion

3 tablespoons vegetable oil

2 tablespoons minced garlic

1 tablespoon chili powder

1 teaspoon ground cumin

1 teaspoon salt

1 teaspoon freshly ground black pepper

12 corn tortillas

Guacamole (page 151), sour cream, salsa, grated cheese, for garnishes

1. Slice the chicken, bell peppers, and onions into thin slices. In a large skillet, heat the oil over medium-high heat. Add the chicken, bell peppers, onions, garlic, chili powder, cumin, salt, and pepper and cook, stirring frequently, until the chicken is fully cooked, 10 to 12 minutes.

2. Fill the tortillas with the chicken-and-peppers mixture. Put the various garnishes in serving bowls and allow everyone to garnish their own fajitas.

VEGETARIAN OPTION

Just leave out the chicken and use extra vegetables! Consider adding mushrooms, zucchini, and squash.

Tamales

Of all the recipes in this book, this is one of the five I am most excited about. Before working on this book, I had purchased tamales many times, but I had never made them myself. Little did I know that they were so easy to prepare and tasted so much better homemade and perfectly fresh than the ones I'd been buying. Best of all, this is one of the cheapest dinners you can make! You'll find corn husks in the ethnic-foods aisle of your local grocery store, typically near the masa flour.

MAKES 8 TAMALES

FOR THE CORN HUSKS AND DOUGH

8 large corn husks

1 gallon water

3 cups masa (corn flour)

1½ cups water

1 cup chicken stock

1 tablespoon butter, melted

2 teaspoons salt

2 teaspoons vegetable oil

FOR THE FILLING AND SERVING

2 tablespoons olive oil

1 cup diced yellow onion

1 garlic clove, minced

1 pound ground beef
(can substitute ground turkey or ground chicken)

FOR THE CORN HUSKS AND DOUGH

1. In a large bowl, soak corn husks in the gallon of water for 2 to 3 hours to soften.

2. In the bowl of a stand mixer, combine the masa, 1½ cups water, stock, butter, salt, and vegetable oil and mix on medium speed until a smooth dough forms. Add additional water as needed and mix to make a pasty dough.

FOR THE FILLING AND SERVING

1. In a large sauté pan, heat the olive oil over medium-high heat. Add the onions and garlic and cook, stirring frequently, until lightly browned, 5 to 7 minutes. Add the beef, chili powder, cumin, paprika, and salt; mix together well, and cook for 1 to 2 minutes. Add the 2 cups water (or enough to just cover the meat) and cook, stirring constantly, until the beef is fully cooked, no pink spots remaining, 10 to 12 minutes.

2. Smear the masa dough generously onto each softened corn husk, coating all the way to the edges. Add 2 table-

1 tablespoon chili powder

1 tablespoon ground cumin

1 tablespoon paprika

1 teaspoon salt

1 to 2 cups water

Accompaniments: Guacamole (page 151), salsa, sour cream

spoons of the meat to the center of dough. Roll up the corn husk, fold over ends so the dough encloses the meat.

3. Bring a large pot of water to a boil, then lower to a simmer. Place the tamales in a steamer basket over the pot and steam them until the corn husks easily pull away from the dough, about 40 minutes.

4. Serve with the guacamole, salsa, and sour cream.

Ideas for Other Fillings

USE APPROXIMATELY
1 POUND OF EACH

- Cheese

- Grilled steak or chicken

- Peppers

- Refried beans

- Vegetables (grilled zucchini, squash, onions, red and green bell peppers, etc.)

Empanadas

Empanadas are another one of my favorite recipes. Most restaurants use a pie crust or pastry dough to make their empanadas, so it was something of a challenge to convert the typical crust into a gluten-free alternative. My solution was to use a combination of corn flour, cheese, and grated onions. The flavor is delicious, and the texture is perfect. This recipes uses ground beef for the filling, but you can try ground turkey or chicken or refried beans and cheese.

**MAKES
8 EMPANADAS**

FOR THE DOUGH

2 cups grated sharp cheddar cheese

1 cup very finely grated yellow onion

4 tablespoons butter

2 large eggs

2 cups masa (corn flour)

1 tablespoon xanthan gum

2 teaspoons salt

1 cup water

FOR THE DOUGH

1. Preheat the oven to 400°F.

2. In the bowl of a stand mixer, cream together the cheese, onions, butter, and eggs on medium speed for about 3 to 4 minutes. Add the masa, xanthan gum, and salt and mix well. The mixture will be very crumbly. Slowly add the water until a solid ball of dough forms.

3. Remove the dough from the mixer and form into 8 equal-sized pieces. Pour extra masa onto the work surface and roll each piece of dough into a circle about ¼ inch thick. Place each piece of rolled-out dough onto a greased baking sheet. Set aside until the filling is ready.

2 tablespoons olive oil

1 cup diced yellow onion

1 garlic clove, minced

1 pound ground beef (or
   substitute ground turkey
   or ground chicken)

1 tablespoon chili powder

1 tablespoon ground cumin

1 tablespoon paprika

1 teaspoon salt

1 to 2 cups water

Accompaniments: Guacamole
   (page 151), salsa, sour
   cream

FOR THE FILLING AND ASSEMBLY

1. In a large sauté pan, heat the oil over medium-high heat. Add the onions and garlic and cook, stirring frequently, until lightly browned, 5 to 7 minutes. Add the beef, chili powder, cumin, paprika, and salt, mix together well, and cook for a minute or two. Add the water (just enough to cover the meat) and cook, stirring constantly, until the beef is fully cooked, no pink spots remaining, 10 to 12 minutes.

2. Place 2 tablespoons of the meat in the center of each dough circle. Fold the dough in half to create a pocket. Press your fingers into the dough to seal it closed. Cut 2 small slits in the top of each empanada for venting during cooking.

3. Transfer the empanadas to a baking sheet and bake for 15 minutes. Remove from the oven and serve hot with the guacamole, salsa, and sour cream.

Tacos: Beef, Chicken, Seafood, or Vegetable

Taco night was the best night of the week when I was a kid. My mom used to make a huge platter with all of the best fixings—guacamole, sour cream, lettuce, tomatoes, beans, homemade salsa. It makes my mouth water just thinking about it! This is a basic recipe, so be creative and fix your tacos the way you like them!

MAKES 12 TACOS

FOR THE BEEF TACOS

2 tablespoons olive oil

1 cup diced yellow onion

1 garlic clove, minced

1 pound ground beef

1 tablespoon chili powder

1 tablespoon ground cumin

1 tablespoon paprika

1 teaspoon salt

1 to 2 cups water

12 corn tortillas

Beef Tacos

1. In a large sauté pan, heat the oil over medium-high heat. Add the onions and garlic and cook, stirring frequently, until lightly browned, 5 to 7 minutes. Add the beef, chili powder, cumin, paprika, and salt, mix together well, and cook for 1 to 2 minutes. Add the water (just enough to cover the meat) and cook, stirring constantly until the beef is fully cooked, no pink spots remaining, 10 to 12 minutes.

2. Heat the tortillas and place the beef in the center of each. Top with the tomatoes, lettuce, cheese, sour cream, Pico de Gallo, diced onions, and guacamole. Serve with the refried beans.

FOR THE CHICKEN TACOS

2 tablespoons olive oil

1 cup diced yellow onion

1 garlic clove, minced

3 boneless, skinless chicken breasts, cubed (about 1 pound)

1 tablespoon chili powder

1 tablespoon ground cumin

1 tablespoon paprika

1 teaspoon salt

½ cup water

12 corn tortillas

Chicken Tacos

1. In a large sauté pan, heat the oil over medium-high heat. Add the onions and garlic and cook, stirring frequently, until lightly browned, 5 to 7 minutes. Add the chicken, chili powder, cumin, paprika, and salt, mix together well, and cook for 1 to 2 minutes. Add the water and cook, stirring frequently, until the chicken is fully cooked, 10 to 12 minutes.

2. Heat the tortillas and place chicken in the center of each. Top with the tomatoes, lettuce, cheese, sour cream, Pico de Gallo, diced onions, and guacamole. Serve with the refried beans.

3 tablespoons olive oil

1 cup diced yellow onion

1 garlic clove, minced

½ pound medium shrimp, peeled and deveined

½ pound bay or sea scallops

1 tablespoon chili powder

1 tablespoon ground cumin

1 tablespoon paprika

1 teaspoon salt

12 corn tortillas

3 tablespoons olive oil

1 cup diced yellow onion

1 garlic clove, minced

2 green bell peppers, sliced

2 red bell peppers, sliced

1 zucchini, chopped

1 yellow squash, chopped

1 tablespoon chili powder

1 tablespoon ground cumin

1 tablespoon paprika

1 teaspoon salt

12 corn tortillas

Seafood Tacos

1. In a large sauté pan, heat the oil over medium-high heat. Add the onions and garlic and cook, stirring frequently, until lightly browned. Add the shrimp, scallops, chili powder, cumin, paprika, and salt and cook, stirring frequently, until the shrimp turn pink and the scallops have a sear, 4 to 5 minutes.

2. Heat the tortillas and place the seafood in the center of each. Top with the tomatoes, lettuce, cheese, sour cream, Pico de Gallo, diced onions, and guacamole. Serve with the refried beans.

Vegetable Tacos

1. In a large sauté pan, heat the oil over medium-high heat. Add the onions and garlic and cook, stirring frequently, until lightly browned. Add the bell peppers, zucchini, squash, chili powder, cumin, paprika, and salt and cook, stirring frequently, until the vegetables are tender and cooked, about 5 minutes.

2. Heat the tortillas and place the vegetables in the center of each. Top with the tomatoes, lettuce, cheese, sour cream, Pico de Gallo, diced onions, and guacamole. Serve with the refried beans.

TOPPINGS AND ACCOMPANIMENTS FOR TACOS

Diced tomatoes

Chopped lettuce

Grated cheese (cheddar, Monterey Jack, or Manchego)

Sour cream

Pico de Gallo (page 161)

Diced onions

Guacamole (page 151)

Refried beans

Nachos

Nachos are a great standby meal for a busy day. They take only a few minutes to make and can be simple, with just cheese, or even better loaded with beef, beans, guacamole, and sour cream.

MAKES
4 SERVINGS

FOR THE BEEF

2 tablespoons olive oil

1 cup diced yellow onion

1 garlic clove, minced

1 pound ground beef

1 tablespoon chili powder

1 tablespoon ground cumin

1 tablespoon paprika

1 teaspoon salt

1 to 2 cups water

FOR THE NACHOS

4 cups corn chips

½ cup refried beans

1 cup grated cheddar cheese

1 cup grated Monterey Jack cheese

1 tablespoon sour cream

2 tablespoons Guacamole (page 151)

½ cup Pico de Gallo (page 161)

1. Preheat the oven to 400°F.

FOR THE BEEF

1. In a large sauté pan, heat the oil over medium-high heat. Add the onions and garlic and cook, stirring frequently, until lightly browned, 5 to 7 minutes. Add the beef, chili powder, cumin, paprika, and salt, mix together well, and cook for 1 to 2 minutes. Add the water (just enough to cover the meat) and cook, stirring constantly, until the beef is fully cooked, no pink spots remaining, 10 to 12 minutes.

FOR THE NACHOS

1. Arrange the chips on a baking sheet. Top with the beef, refried beans, and cheeses. Bake for 10 minutes, or until the cheese is completely melted. Move the nachos to a plate and top with the sour cream, Guacamole, and Pico de Gallo.

Mango Chicken Quesadillas

I love the combination of the grilled chicken and the fresh mango. You can substitute seafood or vegetables for the chicken. And you can cook quesadillas in a frying pan or skillet.

MAKES
4 SERVINGS

4 boneless skinless chicken breasts (about 1 ½ pounds total)

Salt and freshly ground black pepper

1 large mango, diced

1 tomato, diced

1 red onion, diced

1 cup finely chopped fresh cilantro

1 tablespoon minced garlic

¼ cup lime juice

8 corn tortillas

2 cups grated Monterey Jack cheese

1. Preheat a grill or a grill pan. Season the chicken with salt and pepper and cook for about 7 minutes on each side.

2. Preheat the oven to 350°F.

3. In a small bowl, combine the mango, tomatoes, onions, cilantro, garlic, and lime juice, and mix together well.

4. Slice the grilled chicken into long strips. Arrange 4 tortillas on a baking sheet and place heaping spoonfuls of the mango mixture onto each tortilla. Add the strips of chicken. Sprinkle the cheese over the chicken. Place a tortilla on top of each stack of ingredients.

5. Bake the quesadillas for 10 to 12 minutes, until the cheese is melted. Cut into wedges and serve.

Taquitos

These taquitos are crunchy on the outside and juicy on the inside.

MAKES
4 SERVINGS

● DAIRY-FREE

2 tablespoons olive oil

1 cup diced yellow onion

1 garlic clove, minced

1 pound ground beef

1 tablespoon chili powder

1 tablespoon ground cumin

1 tablespoon paprika

1 teaspoon salt

1 to 2 cups water

5 cups vegetable oil, for frying

12 corn tortillas

Toothpicks

Sour cream, black beans, and
salsa, for serving

1. In a large sauté pan, heat the olive oil over medium-high heat. Add the onions and garlic and cook, stirring frequently, until lightly browned, 5 to 7 minutes. Add the beef, chili powder, cumin, paprika, and salt and mix together well. Add the water (just enough to cover the meat) and cook, stirring constantly, until the beef is fully cooked, no pink spots remaining, 10 to 12 minutes.

2. In a clean large skillet, heat the vegetable oil over medium-high heat; it's hot enough when you see small bubbles forming in the pan. One at a time, add the tortillas for 2 to 3 seconds, just to get them soft. Place the cooked tortillas on paper towels to absorb any extra oil.

3. Fill each tortilla with 1 tablespoon of the beef. Roll the tortillas up and hold them together with toothpicks. Place the taquitos back into the hot oil and fry until golden brown. Do not overfry; you want the taquitos to remain soft.

4. Serve with the sour cream, black beans, and salsa.

Grilled Halloumi on a Bed of Peach Salsa and Avocado

This is a vegetarian winner filled with amazing flavors! The halloumi cheese is salty and firmly textured, making it perfect for the grill.

MAKES
4 SERVINGS

■ VEGETARIAN

FOR THE SALSA

2 cups fresh peaches, peeled and chopped

1 cup diced tomato

¼ cup chopped fresh cilantro

¼ cup chopped red onion

3 tablespoons lime juice

1 tablespoon finely chopped serrano chile (seeds removed)

1 garlic clove, minced

FOR THE SALAD

16 ounces halloumi cheese

1 tablespoon extra-virgin olive oil

Salt and freshly ground black pepper

1 ripe avocado

FOR THE SALSA

1. In a medium bowl, stir together the peaches, tomatoes, cilantro, onions, lime juice, chile, and garlic. Chill the salsa before serving.

FOR THE SALAD

1. Preheat the grill or a grill pan. Slice the cheese into four equal-sized pieces. Rub a small amount of the oil all over the cheese. Season with the salt and pepper. Grill the cheese for 3 minutes on each side.

2. Spoon 1-cup portions of the salsa onto each plate. Cut open the avocado, remove the pit, and slice it lengthwise. Lay slices on the salsa. Place the grilled cheese on top of the avocado slices and serve.

Carne Asada and Creamy Potato Puree

This recipe comes from the kitchen of Chef Edgar Steele of Café Atlantico. It is a terrific Nuevo-Latino version of a classic carne asada.

FOR THE STEAK

1 mango, peeled and cut into chunks

1 small red onion, diced

½ cup fresh orange juice

¼ cup canola oil

1 garlic clove, minced

2 tablespoons finely chopped canned chipotle peppers in adobo sauce

1 tablespoon dried thyme

2 teaspoons black peppercorns

1 teaspoon salt

2 pounds skirt steak, cut into 8 4-ounce portions

FOR THE POTATOES

2 large Idaho potatoes, peeled and cut lengthwise into quarters

½ cup heavy cream, warmed in microwave or on stove

2 teaspoons butter

Salt

FOR THE STEAK

1. In a blender, place the mango, onions, juice, oil, garlic, chipotle peppers, thyme, peppercorns, and salt and blend on high speed until pureed into a smooth sauce. In a large bowl, cover the steak with the mixture, refrigerate, and marinate for at least 2 hours.

FOR THE POTATOES

1. In a large saucepan, place the potatoes and barely cover them with water. Cover the pot and bring to a boil over medium-high heat. Cook the potatoes until tender, about 20 minutes.

2. Remove the pot from the heat and add the cream. Puree the potatoes with a hand blender until smooth and free of lumps; it is important to work with the potatoes while they are hot to avoid a gluey consistency. Whisk in the butter and salt to taste and keep the potatoes warm.

TO FINISH

1. Preheat the grill or a grill pan. Remove the steaks from the marinade, season with salt, and grill to the desired doneness, 3 to 4 minutes per side for medium-rare. Serve the grilled steak over the potato puree.

Sautéed Shrimp and Scallops with Tomato Stew

This warm and hearty dish comes from the kitchen of Chef Edgar Steele of Café Atlantico. It is perfect for a cold night.

MAKES
4 SERVINGS

2 tablespoons butter

3 cups diced yellow onion

1½ cups diced green bell pepper

1 fresh bay leaf

3 cups cored, seeded, and diced (¼-inch cubes) tomatoes (cores reserved)

2 tablespoons coconut milk

1 tablespoon chopped fresh tarragon

Sea salt

12 medium shrimp, peeled and deveined

8 large scallops

1 tablespoon extra-virgin olive oil

16 chive tips, about 2½ inches in length, for garnish

1. In a medium sauté pan, heat the butter over low heat. Add the onions, bell peppers, and bay leaf and cook, stirring, until the onions are translucent and beginning to caramelize, about 30 minutes. Remove the bay leaf from the pan.

2. In a blender, puree the reserved cores of the tomatoes on high speed.

3. Add the pureed tomato cores and the diced tomatoes to the pan and simmer until reduced to a "jam" consistency, about 8 minutes. Add the coconut milk and tarragon and bring to a simmer. Cook for 5 minutes longer, adjust the seasoning with salt and keep the mixture warm.

4. Season the shrimp and scallops with salt. In a large sauté pan, heat the oil over medium-high heat and add the shrimp. Cook the shrimp quickly on both sides, stirring frequently, just until they are pink and cooked through, 3 to 4 minutes.

5. Remove the shrimp from the pan and cook the scallops on each side until they are golden and can easily be lifted, 2 to 3 minutes per side. To serve, place some of the tomato mixture on each plate and randomly place the shrimp and scallops on top. Garnish with the chive tips.

Tequila Shrimp with Garlic, Chiles, and Cilantro Rice

This recipe comes from the kitchen of Chef Edgar Steele of Café Atlantico. The rice is full of luscious flavors and goes well with tequila shrimp or any other protein.

MAKES 4 SERVINGS

FOR THE RICE

1 cup white rice

1¼ cups water

1 teaspoon butter

1 fresh bay leaf

1 teaspoon salt

2 tablespoons finely chopped fresh cilantro

FOR THE SHRIMP

2 tablespoons extra-virgin olive oil

3 garlic cloves, finely sliced

3 piquillo chiles, thinly sliced (or substitute 1 red bell pepper)

24 small shrimp, peeled and deveined

2 ounces tequila

Salt

FOR THE RICE

1. Place the rice in a strainer and rinse under cold running water until the water runs clear. In a small saucepan, combine the rice with the water, butter, bay leaf, and salt. Cover the pot and place over medium-high heat. When it starts to boil, reduce the heat to low and cook, stirring often to prevent burning, until tender, 20 to 25 minutes. Remove the bay leaf and gently toss in the cilantro. Cover the rice and keep it warm.

FOR THE SHRIMP

1. In a large sauté pan, heat the oil over medium-high heat. Add the garlic and cook, stirring frequently, until golden, 1 to 2 minutes. Add the chile and cook, stirring frequently, until softened, 3 to 4 minutes.

2. Add the shrimp and cook, stirring frequently, for 30 seconds. Carefully add the tequila to the pan and stand back; the alcohol in the tequila will flame up as it burns away! Allow the shrimp to fully cook, for 5 to 6 minutes. Add salt to taste.

3. To serve, place a mound of rice on each plate and place the shrimp with some of the garlic-chile sauce on top.

Grilled Salmon with Avocado-Cilantro Cream, Fresh Mango, and Jasmine Rice

The name of this dish makes it sound very complicated, but when you get to the kitchen to make it, you'll find that it is actually quite simple. The tropical flavors of the mango bring out the best in the avocado cream sauce and the salmon. I promise, you'll want to go back for seconds!

**MAKES
4 SERVINGS**

2 cups jasmine rice

2 large ripe avocados, peeled and pitted

1 cup diced red onion

1 cup fresh cilantro leaves

2 tablespoons heavy cream

1 tablespoon minced garlic

1 teaspoon salt

4 salmon fillets (about 1 pound total)

Salt and freshly ground black pepper

1 large ripe mango, peeled, sliced, and cut into strips

1. Cook the rice according to the package instructions.

2. In a food processor, combine the avocado, onions, cilantro, cream, garlic, and salt and puree until a smooth mixture is formed.

3. Preheat the grill or a grill pan. Season the salmon with salt and pepper and grill for 4 to 5 minutes on each side, or until the desired doneness is reached.

4. Place ½ cup of rice on each plate. Put a salmon fillet on the rice and top with a generous portion of the avocado-cilantro cream sauce. Lay strips of the mango on top of the sauce before serving.

Red Snapper with Fresh Peach Salsa and Quinoa

Quinoa is a fantastic substitute for rice and a nutrition powerhouse. With this recipe you're getting essential vitamins and delicious flavors! I like to leave the skin on the peaches, but if you don't like the texture, then peel the peaches before adding them to the salsa.

MAKES
4 SERVINGS

● DAIRY-FREE

1½ cups quinoa

2 cups diced peaches

1 cup chopped fresh cilantro

¼ cup chopped red onion

3 tablespoons fresh lime juice

1 tablespoon finely chopped serrano chile (seeds removed)

1 garlic clove, minced

Salt

4 fillets red snapper (about 1 pound total)

Olive oil, for brushing

Salt and freshly ground black pepper

1. Cook the quinoa according to the package instructions.

2. In a small bowl, stir together the peaches, cilantro, onions, lime juice, chile, and garlic. Season with the salt to taste.

3. Preheat the grill or a grill pan. Brush the snapper with the oil and season with the salt and pepper. Grill for 3 to 4 minutes on each side.

4. Spoon 1-cup portions of quinoa onto each plate. Place the fish on the quinoa and top each with a generous portion of the peach salsa.

Papaya-Cilantro Salmon with Coconut Rice

The coconut milk is fully absorbed into the rice and makes for a fabulous creamy dish. The papaya-cilantro puree cuts the coconut sweetness for the perfect balance of flavors. If your grocery store doesn't have papayas, substitute peaches.

MAKES
4 SERVINGS

● DAIRY-FREE

6 tablespoons olive oil

2 cups white rice

3 cups coconut milk

2 cups chicken stock

2 cups peeled and diced papaya

½ cup chopped fresh cilantro

¼ cup roughly chopped red onion

3 tablespoons fresh lime juice

1 garlic clove

1½ teaspoons salt

4 salmon steaks (about 1 pound total)

1 teaspoon freshly ground black pepper

1. In a medium saucepan, heat 3 tablespoons of the oil over medium-high heat. Add the rice and cook, stirring to coat well, for 2 to 3 minutes. Add the coconut milk and stock and bring to a boil. Reduce the heat and simmer, stirring constantly, until the liquid is fully absorbed, about 18 minutes.

2. In a food processor, combine the papaya, cilantro, onions, lime juice, garlic, and ½ teaspoon of the salt and process into a smooth sauce. Set aside.

3. Preheat the grill or a grill pan. Brush the salmon steaks with the remaining 3 tablespoons of oil and season with the remaining salt and the pepper. Grill the salmon for 4 to 5 minutes on each side.

4. Spoon the rice into bowls. Place the salmon steaks on the rice and top with generous portions of the papaya puree.

Grilled Chicken with Avocado Salsa

This recipe comes from the kitchen of Chef Edgar Steele of Café Atlantico. You'll love the wonderful play between bright fruit flavors and the savory grilled meat.

● DAIRY-FREE

FOR THE CHICKEN

1 cup orange juice

1 lime, cut into quarters, seeds removed

2 garlic cloves

2 tablespoons extra-virgin olive oil

2 tablespoons finely sliced scallions, plus extra for garnish

1 tablespoon chopped canned chipotle peppers in adobo sauce (reserve sauce)

1 tablespoon chopped serrano chile

1 tablespoon maple syrup

1 tablespoon paprika

1 tablespoon salt

1 tablespoon sherry vinegar

2 teaspoons chopped fresh rosemary

Sea salt

8 boneless, skinless chicken breasts (about 3 pounds total)

FOR THE CHICKEN

1. The day before you plan to serve the dish, in a blender, combine the juice, lime, garlic, oil, scallions, chipotle peppers, chile, maple syrup, paprika, salt, vinegar, and rosemary and blend on high speed until smooth. Place the chicken in a glass dish and completely cover it with the mixture. Cover with plastic wrap and allow the chicken to marinate in the refrigerator for 24 hours.

FOR THE AVOCADO SALSA

1. Preheat the grill or a grill pan. Cut the onion into 3/4-inch slices. Coat the onion, avocados, tomatoes, chile, and garlic with 2 tablespoons of the oil and season with the salt. Place the oiled vegetables on the grill and cook until the grill marks have formed and the vegetables are slightly charred. Turn them over to get grill marks on both sides. (If you are using a grill, it is best to use one with grill bars that are close together to prevent small pieces of the onion and garlic from falling through. If the grill bars are not close together, pierce a piece of aluminum foil in several places with a knife, and lay the smaller vegetables on the foil.) Remove the vegetables from the grill and allow to cool.

1 small red onion

2 whole unpeeled ripe
   avocados, pitted and halved

2 plum tomatoes

1 small serrano chile

1 garlic clove, sliced

3 tablespoons extra-virgin
   olive oil

Salt

1 teaspoon fresh lime juice

1 teaspoon orange juice

1 teaspoon sugar

Zest of ½ lime

¾ teaspoon finely chopped
   fresh rosemary (chopped
   to a powder)

Sliced scallions, for garnish

2. Remove the skin from the avocados and dice the flesh into ½-inch chunks. Dice the onions and tomatoes into equal-sized chunks. Remove the stem, core, and seeds from the chile and dice it into very fine pieces. Thinly slice the garlic.

3. In a large bowl, place all the grilled vegetables, lime juice, the orange juice, sugar, lime zest, and rosemary. Gently toss the ingredients, add salt to taste, and keep the vegetables warm.

4. Remove the chicken from the marinade. Season each breast with salt and grill until completely cooked, 8 to 10 minutes on each side.

5. To serve, place some of the salsa on each plate and top with the grilled chicken. Garnish with sliced scallions.

Grilled Sea Bass with Pico de Gallo and Brown Rice

This simple, healthful dish stars brown rice. It contains important vitamins such as B1, B3, magnesium, and iron that are not found in white rice. You can substitute brown rice in any rice recipe in this book.

MAKES
4 SERVINGS

● DAIRY-FREE

FOR THE SEA BASS AND RICE

1½ cups brown rice

One 2-pound piece sea bass

Salt and freshly ground black pepper

FOR THE PICO DE GALLO

6 large tomatoes, diced

1 medium onion, diced

2 to 4 fresh serrano chiles, seeded and finely diced

½ cup chopped fresh cilantro

¼ cup fresh lime juice

1 teaspoon garlic powder

Salt and freshly ground black pepper

FOR THE SEA BASS AND RICE

1. Cook the brown rice according to the package instructions.

2. Preheat the grill or a grill pan. Season the sea bass with salt and pepper. Cook the fish for 5 to 6 minutes on each side. Cut into four equal-sized pieces.

FOR THE PICO DE GALLO

1. In a large bowl, combine the tomatoes, onions, chile, cilantro, juice, and garlic powder. Add salt and pepper to taste.

2. Place a heaping portion of rice on each plate. Top each with a piece of sea bass and top the sea bass with pico de gallo.

Strip Steak with Black Beans, Corn, and Cilantro

I love a good strip steak, especially when it is loaded with garnishes. This is a quick and simple recipe perfect for a busy day.

MAKES
4 SERVINGS

● DAIRY-FREE

2 tablespoons gluten-free soy sauce

1 tablespoon minced garlic

1 tablespoon olive oil

4 strip steaks (about 1 pound total)

2 cups drained canned black beans

1 cup chopped fresh cilantro

1 cup diced tomatoes

1 cup frozen yellow corn kernels, thawed

½ cup finely diced yellow onion

¼ cup fresh lime juice

1 tablespoon very finely diced jalapeño chile (seeds removed)

Salt and freshly ground black pepper

1. Preheat the grill or a grill pan. In a small bowl, whisk together the soy sauce, garlic, and oil. Spread the mixture over the steaks and marinate for 30 minutes. Grill the steaks to the desired doneness, 4 to 5 minutes per side for medium-rare.

2. Meanwhile, in a medium bowl, combine the black beans, cilantro, tomatoes, corn, onions, juice, and chile. Season with the salt and pepper.

3. Remove the steaks from the grill and place on plates. Serve the black-bean-and-corn mixture on top.

GLUTEN-FREE
Desserts

Dessert is arguably my favorite part of the meal. It brings the entire meal to a close and leaves you feeling completely satisfied. My favorite part about eating gluten-free desserts is when my family and friends eat the dessert and their eyes pop and they say, "Oh my goodness . . . this can't be gluten-free!" The recipes ahead are that good and will make everyone believe that gluten-free is an amazing way to cook!

But before we get into cooking, there are a few things you need to remember about gluten-free baking. There are no one-to-one substitutes for wheat flour in baked goods. This is largely because gluten is the ingredient that makes your dough or batter stretchy and elastic. Depending on how much water you add or how long you work with the dough, the gluten is responsible for reaching your desired consistency. For example, when you make a pie crust, you'll use very little water and mix for a very short time because you want a flaky texture. When you bake bread, you'll add more water and knead the dough to make it chewy.

When you remove the gluten from your flour mix, you have to find a replacement for the missing protein in order to reach the right firmness and consistency in your baked goods. To do this, you must use a combination of flours and add gums. No, I don't mean chewing gum! I'm talking about guar gum or xanthan gum. These ingredients are used as stabilizers and will add viscosity or thickness to your baked goods. But be careful not to add too much! When baking, you'll want to stick to about ⅓ teaspoon per cup of flour to prevent the texture of your cake or pastry from becoming clumpy.

On the next page is my own recipe for an all-purpose gluten-free flour mix.

Vanessa's All-Purpose Flour Mix

This recipe works well with breads, cakes, pie crusts, and most other baked goods.

MAKES
ABOUT 3 CUPS

● DAIRY-FREE
▪ VEGETARIAN

2 cups brown rice flour

¾ cup cornstarch

2 tablespoons tapioca flour

1 teaspoon xanthan gum

1. Gently mix all ingredients together and use as a one-to-one substitute in recipes that call for wheat flour.

So now that you know all about making a gluten-free flour mix, you're almost ready to start making dessert. But there's one more point I want to make before we get to the kitchen. Not all desserts need to use flour. In fact, some of the most delicious ones can be made using no flour at all. Try making a cheesecake using crushed nuts for the crust or caramelizing fruit and topping it with ice cream. These desserts are naturally gluten-free and simple to make!

Now on to dessert!

DESSERT INGREDIENTS *to Keep in Your Kitchen*

After trying the recipes in this chapter, you'll be a pro at cooking gluten-free desserts! Each recipe ahead uses naturally gluten-free flours, fruits, dairy products, and sugars to make the most delicious desserts. Having all the right ingredients in your pantry will help you quickly adapt to baking gluten-free goodies. You'll want to keep on hand a variety of gluten-free flours, the baking staples, and of course, the best fresh fruits you can find.

FLOURS

I always purchase Bob's Red Mill (www.bobsredmill.com) brand flours and grains because the company certifies on their packaging that each item was produced in a facility that is free of any gluten-containing ingredients. For rice, I generally purchase Lundberg (www.lundberg.com) or Rice Select (www.riceselect.com) brands because both companies have information available about the gluten-free status of their products.

Brown rice flour

Cornstarch

Potato starch

Quinoa

Soy flour

Tapioca flour

White rice (long grain)

White rice flour

Xanthan gum

FRUITS FOR DESSERTS

I love making cobblers, pies, and other sweet desserts that are based around the sweetest fruits. They can be served hot and steaming in the winter or topped with ice cream for a light refreshing dessert in the summer. Here are some of my favorite fruits to make desserts with.

Apples

Bananas

Cherries

Mangoes

Peaches

Raspberries

OTHER INGREDIENTS

Many of the ingredients used in regular baking can still be used in gluten-free baking. These staples are naturally gluten-free and will help form the texture and shape of your gluten-free baked goods.

Baking powder

Baking soda

Brown sugar
(light and dark)

Chocolate chips

Cinnamon

Cocoa powder

Eggs

Food coloring

Granulated sugar

Milk

Nuts

Vanilla extract

Apple-Blueberry-Walnut Crisp

MAKES
6 SERVINGS

■ VEGETARIAN

This is a fresh and fruity crisp that is fabulous when served with a large scoop of vanilla ice cream on top.

1. Preheat the oven to 350°F.

FOR THE FRUIT FILLING

6 Granny Smith apples, peeled, cored, and sliced

2 cups blueberries

1 cup chopped walnuts

1 cup granulated sugar

1 cup packed light brown sugar

4 tablespoons unsalted butter, melted

¼ cup brown rice flour

1 tablespoon ground cinnamon

1 teaspoon ground nutmeg

FOR THE CINNAMON CRUNCH TOPPING

1 cup packed light brown sugar

½ cup granulated sugar

¾ cup Bob's Red Mill gluten-free oats

½ cup finely chopped walnuts

¼ cup brown rice flour

¼ cup tapioca flour

¼ cup cornstarch

2 tablespoons ground cinnamon

8 tablespoons unsalted butter, melted

FOR THE FRUIT FILLING

1. In a large bowl, combine the apples, blueberries, walnuts, both sugars, melted butter, brown rice flour, cinnamon, and nutmeg. Stir well and pour into a 9 x 13-inch ungreased glass baking dish. Set aside.

FOR THE CINNAMON CRUNCH TOPPING

1. In a large bowl, combine the sugars, oats, walnuts, flours, cornstarch, and cinnamon. Pour the melted butter over the dry ingredients and mix together with your hands to form moist clumps.

2. Sprinkle the crunch mixture evenly over the top of the fruit and bake for 45 minutes. Serve hot or warm. Store any leftover cobbler in an airtight container in the refrigerator for up to 1 week and reheat in the microwave.

Bananas Foster

This is a fancy dessert that anyone can make!

MAKES
4 SERVINGS

VEGETARIAN

½ cup packed light brown sugar

¼ cup dark rum

2 tablespoons unsalted butter

2 bananas, sliced in half lengthwise

1 pint vanilla ice cream

1. In a medium skillet, heat the sugar, rum, and butter over medium heat, stirring frequently. When the mixture begins to bubble, add the bananas. Gently swirl the bananas in the sugar mixture for about 4 to 5 minutes until the sugar begins to caramelize.

2. Scoop ice cream into bowls and top with the bananas and caramelized sauce.

Chocolate Fudge Cake

This is the first gluten-free chocolate cake recipe that I've thought tastes absolutely normal. It takes a lot of ingredients and time to make, but I promise, it is worth it. You'll be so happy the minute you take a bite of this moist, rich, and delicious cake.

MAKES 12 TO 16 SERVINGS

VEGETARIAN

FOR THE CAKE

2 cups brown rice flour

1 cup tapioca flour

½ cup cocoa powder

¼ cup cornstarch

1 tablespoon baking soda

1 teaspoon xanthan gum

1 teaspoon salt

1 cup unsalted butter

1¾ cups packed dark brown sugar

1 cup granulated sugar

1 tablespoon vanilla extract

4 large eggs

1 cup buttermilk

½ cup sour cream

1 cup prepared coffee

½ cup boiling water

FOR THE CAKE

1. Preheat the oven to 350°F. Grease two 9-inch round baking pans with nonstick cooking spray.

2. In a large bowl, combine the flours, cocoa powder, cornstarch, baking soda, xanthan gum, and salt and stir together well. Set aside.

3. In the bowl of a stand mixer, cream together the butter, sugars, and vanilla for 3 to 4 minutes. Add the eggs one at a time, allowing each to mix in thoroughly before adding another. Add the buttermilk and sour cream and mix in well, about 2 minutes.

4. Turn the mixer speed down to low and slowly add the dry ingredients. Mix for about 2 minutes.

5. Add the coffee and boiling water and mix slowly for about 2 more minutes. Pour the batter into the prepared pans. Bake for 30 to 35 minutes, or until a toothpick inserted in the center of the cake comes out clean. Allow the cake to cool in the pans for 5 minutes, then turn the cakes out onto racks to cool completely before frosting.

**FOR THE CHOCOLATE
BUTTERCREAM FROSTING**

½ cup semisweet chocolate
   chips, melted

1 pound powdered sugar

2 tablespoons unsalted butter

1 teaspoon vanilla extract

3 tablespoons milk

FOR THE CHOCOLATE BUTTERCREAM FROSTING

1. In a food processor, combine the chocolate, sugar, butter, and vanilla. With the food processor running, slowly add the milk until the frosting reaches the desired consistency.

2. First frost the top of one cake layer. Lay the second cake layer on top. Frost the top and sides of the entire cake. Chill briefly to set the frosting, then serve!

3. Store leftover cake in an airtight container in the refrigerator for up to 1 week. You can freeze the cake for up to 1 month. Defrost the frozen cake at room temperature before serving.

Double Chocolate Chip Cookies

Soft, chewy, and filled with amazing flavors, these are my all-time favorite cookies. I love the combination of milk chocolate and white chocolate, and the pecans add great crunchiness.

MAKES 3
DOZEN COOKIES

■ VEGETARIAN

1¼ cups packed dark brown sugar

1 cup unsalted butter, melted

¼ cup granulated sugar

1 large egg

1 large egg white

2 tablespoons nonfat vanilla-flavored creamer (such as Coffeemate)

2 teaspoons vanilla extract

2 cups brown rice flour

2 tablespoons tapioca flour

¼ cup cornstarch (can use potato starch)

1 teaspoon baking soda

1 teaspoon salt

1 teaspoon xanthan gum

1 cup milk chocolate chips

1 cup white chocolate chips

½ cup pecans, chopped

1. Preheat the oven to 375°F. Grease 2 baking sheets with nonstick cooking spray.

2. In the bowl of a stand mixer, cream together the sugars, melted butter, whole egg, egg white, vanilla-flavored creamer, and vanilla, about 3 to 4 minutes.

3. In a separate large bowl, mix together the flours, cornstarch, baking soda, salt, and xanthan gum until evenly blended.

4. Turn the mixer speed down to low and slowly add the dry ingredients to the butter-sugar mixture, mixing until a smooth dough forms, 5 to 6 minutes. Add both the chocolate chips and the pecans and mix just until fully incorporated, about 10 seconds.

5. Form the dough into balls about 2 inches in diameter and place on the prepared baking sheets about one inch apart. Bake for 13 minutes, rotating the pans from top to bottom about halfway through the baking for even doneness. Set the baking sheets on cooling racks to cool for 5 minutes before transferring the cookies to the racks to cool completely.

6. Store leftover cookies unrefrigerated, in an airtight container for up to 1 week. You can also freeze the cookies for up to 2 months.

Peanut Butter–Chocolate Cheesecake

This is the best chocolate–peanut butter cheesecake ever! The simple crust is naturally gluten-free. The filling is rich and creamy. You won't be able to have just one piece.

FOR THE CRUST

1 cup peanut butter

1 large egg

1 cup granulated sugar

FOR THE FILLING

Four 8-ounce packages cream cheese, softened

1 cup granulated sugar

1 teaspoon vanilla extract

1 cup sour cream

4 large eggs

2 cups peanut butter

2 cups semisweet chocolate chips

FOR THE CRUST

1. Preheat the oven to 350°F. Grease a 9-inch springform pan with nonstick cooking spray.

2. In a large bowl, combine the peanut butter, egg, and sugar. Spread onto the bottom of the springform pan. Bake for 8 minutes. Set aside, but leave the oven on.

FOR THE FILLING

1. In a large bowl, beat the cream cheese, sugar, and vanilla with an electric mixer on medium speed until well blended. Add the sour cream and mix well. Add the eggs, one at a time, mixing on low speed after each addition until blended.

2. In a microwave-safe dish, melt the peanut butter and chocolate chips together. Stir into the batter.

3. Pour the batter over the crust and bake for 50 minutes or until the center is almost set. Transfer to a cooling rack to cool in the pan for 45 minutes to an hour. Transfer to the refrigerator to cool completely for 3 to 4 hours. Remove the sides of the springform pan before serving.

4. Store leftovers in an airtight container in the refrigerator for up to 1 week.

Sticky Coconut Rice with Mango

A classic Asian dessert that is fruity, sweet, and delicious.

One 14-ounce can coconut milk

1 cup Japanese-style (short grain) rice

1 cup skim milk

1 cup sweetened shredded coconut

1 cup water

2 tablespoons granulated sugar

1 teaspoon salt

1 mango, peeled and sliced

Mint leaves, for garnish

1. In a medium saucepan, combine the coconut milk, rice, skim milk, shredded coconut, water, sugar, and salt. Cook over medium heat, stirring constantly, until the liquid is mostly absorbed but the rice is still a bit runny, about 20 minutes.

2. Spoon the rice into bowls. Top with sliced mango and garnish with mint leaves. Serve warm, or chill for 2 hours and serve cold.

Coconut Rice Pudding

Coconut milk makes rice pudding even better than the version I loved as a kid. Try topping it with crushed pineapple or mango for a fruity twist. I like to use skim milk in this recipe, but if you're in the mood for a richer dessert, use 2 percent milk or half-and-half.

2 cups white rice

2 cups coconut milk

2 cups skim milk

⅔ cup granulated sugar

½ teaspoon salt

1 cup sweetened shredded coconut

2 large eggs, beaten

2 tablespoons unsalted butter

2½ tablespoons cinnamon sugar (2 tablespoons granulated sugar plus 1½ teaspoons ground cinnamon)

1 teaspoon vanilla extract

1. In a large pot, bring 4 cups of water to a boil. Add the rice, cover, and simmer until most of the liquid is absorbed, about 20 minutes.

2. In a separate large pot, combine the cooked rice, coconut milk, 1 cup of the skim milk, the sugar, and salt. Simmer over medium heat for 20 minutes.

3. Add the remaining 1 cup of skim milk, the shredded coconut, eggs, butter, 1 tablespoon of the cinnamon sugar, and vanilla and simmer until the liquid is almost completely absorbed.

4. Cool for 30 minutes, then transfer to the refrigerator to cool for 1 to 2 hours. Serve in ice cream dishes with a sprinkle of the remaining cinnamon sugar on top. Store leftovers in an airtight container in the refrigerator for up to 1 week.

Pineapple-Coconut Crème Brûlée

To give crème brûlée a kick, I added crushed pineapple and coconut milk. The result is thick and creamy, with a subtle fruitiness that I know you'll love.

VEGETARIAN

One 14-ounce can coconut milk

½ cup skim milk

1 cup canned, crushed pineapple packed in juice, drained

1 cup sweetened shredded coconut

4 large egg yolks

½ cup granulated sugar

1 tablespoon cornstarch

1 teaspoon vanilla extract

¼ cup packed light brown sugar

1. Preheat the oven to 350°F.

2. In a large saucepan, heat the coconut milk and skim milk over medium heat for 5 minutes. Stir in the pineapple and shredded coconut and cook, stirring constantly, until the mixture comes to a boil. Remove from heat.

3. In a large bowl, combine the egg yolks, sugar, cornstarch, and vanilla until a runny paste forms.

4. Remove 1 cup of the hot milk mixture and slowly pour it into the egg yolk paste, mixing well. Pour the mixture of paste and milk back into the pan with the remaining milk mixture. Return the pan to the heat and cook, stirring constantly, until a thick custard forms, about 15 minutes.

5. Set four 6-ounce heatproof dishes in a large roasting pan. Pour the custard into the dishes and carefully fill the roasting pan with water that comes halfway up the sides of the dishes. Bake for 28 to 30 minutes, checking to see that the custard is set.

6. Remove the pan from the oven. Sprinkle brown sugar over the custard.

7. Preheat the broiler.

8. Put the custard dishes under the broiler until the brown sugar forms a crust; this will happen very quickly, so be sure to watch closely to prevent burning.

9. Cool on cooling racks until cool to the touch, then transfer to the refrigerator for 2 to 3 hours before serving. Cover leftovers with foil and store in the refrigerator for up to a week.

Green Tea Ice Cream

Most green tea ice cream recipes call for green tea powder, an ingredient that's hard to find. Mainstream grocery stores rarely carry it. My solution is to use freshly brewed green tea and a dash of food coloring. It looks identical to the color created by the elusive powders.

**MAKES
1 QUART**

VEGETARIAN

2 cups half-and-half
1 cup brewed green tea
1 cup skim milk
½ cup sugar
3 drops green food coloring

1. In a large bowl, whisk the half-and-half, tea, skim milk, sugar, and food coloring together.

2. Pour the mixture into an ice cream maker and follow the manufacturer's instructions.

3. Store in an airtight container in the freezer for up to 1 month.

Green Mochi Cake with Chocolate Buttercream Filling

I was inspired to make this recipe after a trip to Japan. Mochi is a staple dessert there and one I hope to make more common in the United States. My mochi recipe steps it up with the addition of a rich chocolate frosting.

MAKES
10 SERVINGS

▩ VEGETARIAN

FOR THE CAKE

One 14-ounce can coconut milk

2 cups water

2 teaspoons vanilla extract

½ teaspoon green food coloring

1 pound white rice flour

2½ cups granulated sugar

1 teaspoon baking powder

½ cup potato starch, for dusting

FOR THE FROSTING

3 cups powdered sugar

1 cup cocoa

8 tablespoons unsalted butter

¼ cup skim milk

FOR THE CAKE

1. Preheat the oven to 350°F. Grease two 9-inch round baking pans with nonstick cooking spray.

2. In a large bowl, combine the coconut milk, water, vanilla, and food coloring. In a separate large bowl, mix together the flour, sugar, and baking powder. Slowly mix the dry ingredients into the wet ones, making sure there are no lumps of flour.

3. Fill each prepared baking pan with half the mixture. Cover each pan with foil and bake for 1 hour.

4. Remove pans from the oven and turn the mochi out onto a clean surface that has been dusted with potato starch. Allow to cool completely for about 2 hours.

FOR THE FROSTING

1. In a food processor, combine the powdered sugar, cocoa, butter, and skim milk and pulse until a smooth frosting forms. Spread the frosting generously over the top of one cake layer. Place the other cake layer on top. Chill briefly to set frosting. Slice and serve.

2. Store leftover cake in an airtight container in the refrigerator for up to 1 week.

Red Velvet Mochi Cupcakes with Ginger Buttercream Frosting

These cupcakes are bright and full of delicious flavors. The ginger is subtle but just enough to give the melting sweetness a nice edge.

MAKES
24 CUPCAKES

■ VEGETARIAN

FOR THE CUPCAKES

One 14-ounce can coconut milk

2 cups water

½ cup Hershey's chocolate syrup

2 tablespoons red food coloring

2 teaspoons vanilla extract

4 cups white rice flour

2½ cups granulated sugar

½ cup cocoa

1 teaspoon baking powder

FOR THE FROSTING

3 cups powdered sugar

4 tablespoons (½ stick) unsalted butter

¼ cup milk

1 tablespoon ground ginger

1 teaspoon freshly grated lemon zest

1 teaspoon vanilla extract

FOR THE CUPCAKES

1. Preheat the oven to 350°F. Prepare 24 muffin cups with paper liners and grease the inside of each liner lightly with nonstick cooking spray.

2. In a large bowl, combine the coconut milk, water, chocolate syrup, food coloring, and vanilla. In a separate large bowl, mix together the flour, granulated sugar, cocoa, and baking powder. Slowly mix the dry ingredients into the wet ones, making sure there are no lumps of flour.

3. Fill each muffin cup to the top. Cover the pan with foil and bake for 30 to 35 minutes, or until a toothpick inserted comes out clean. Remove from the oven and allow the cupcakes to cool completely.

FOR THE FROSTING

1. In a food processor, combine the powdered sugar, butter, milk, ginger, lemon zest, and vanilla and pulse until a smooth frosting forms. Spread the top of each cupcake with frosting. Chill briefly to set the frosting before serving.

2. Store leftover cupcakes in an airtight container in the refrigerator for up to 1 week. You can also wrap unfrosted cupcakes in foil and freeze them for up to 1 month.

Chocolate-Ginger Bites

These little treasures are bursting with strong ginger flavor. Once you start eating them, you won't be able to stop!

■ VEGETARIAN

FOR THE COOKIES

1 cup unsalted butter

2 tablespoons vegetable oil

1 large egg

1 teaspoon vanilla extract

1½ cups powdered sugar

½ cup cornstarch

⅔ cup tapioca flour

½ cup brown rice flour

½ cup cocoa powder

FOR THE TOPPING

½ cup powdered sugar

2 tablespoons ground ginger

FOR THE COOKIES

1. Preheat the oven to 350°F. Grease 2 cookie sheets with nonstick cooking spray.

2. In the bowl of a stand mixer, cream together the butter, oil, egg, and vanilla.

3. In a separate large bowl, combine the sugar, cornstarch, flours, and cocoa powder. Slowly add the dry mixture to the wet ingredients and mix well.

4. Form the dough into 2-inch balls and place them on the prepared cookie sheet approximately 1 inch apart. Bake for 18 minutes, rotating the pans from top to bottom about halfway through the baking for even doneness.

FOR THE TOPPING

1. While the cookies are baking, in a large bowl, mix the powdered sugar and ginger together. Transfer the cookie sheets to cooling racks. While the cookies are still hot but just cool enough to safely touch, toss them gently in the topping mixture to coat well. Transfer the cookies to cooling racks to cool completely. Serve with milk. Store leftover cookies in an airtight bag for up to 1 week. Freeze in an airtight bag for up to 2 months.

White Chocolate–Mango Cheesecake

This recipe is the most requested dessert among my friends and family. It is creamy and rich, but the mango offsets these decadent qualities and makes it the perfect summer dessert.

MAKES
8 SERVINGS

▪ VEGETARIAN

FOR THE CRUST

2 cups walnut halves

1½ teaspoons ground cinnamon

2 tablespoons granulated sugar

2 tablespoons unsalted butter, melted

FOR THE FILLING

Four 8-ounce packages cream cheese, softened

1 cup sour cream

2 tablespoons ricotta cheese

1 cup granulated sugar

4 large eggs

12 ounces white chocolate, melted

1 teaspoon vanilla extract

FOR THE CRUST

1. Preheat the oven to 350°F.

2. In a food processor, combine the walnuts, cinnamon, sugar, and butter and process until the nuts are finely chopped. Press the mixture into the bottom of an ungreased 9-inch springform pan. Bake for about 10 minutes and set aside. Leave the oven on.

FOR THE FILLING

1. In a food processor, combine the cream cheese, sour cream, and ricotta. With the machine running, slowly add in the sugar and eggs and mix until completely smooth. Add in the melted white chocolate and vanilla.

2. Pour the mixture onto of the crust and bake for 50 minutes, or until the center is almost set. Transfer to a cooling rack to cool in the pan for 45 minutes to an hour. Transfer to the refrigerator to cool completely for 3 to 4 hours.

FOR THE MANGO TOPPING

1 cup water

2 cups granulated sugar

1 tablespoon fresh lime juice

2 cups diced mango

FOR THE MANGO TOPPING

1. In a small saucepan, bring the water to a boil. Add the sugar and lime juice and cook, stirring constantly, until mixture reduces to a simple syrup, 12 to 15 minutes. Remove from the heat and cool the syrup for 2 hours.

2. In a blender, combine the cooled syrup and diced mango. Puree for about 10 seconds. Spoon the mixture on top of the cheesecake. Chill briefly to set the topping. Remove the sides of springform pan before serving.

3. Store leftovers in an airtight container in the refrigerator for up to 1 week.

Apple Fried Ice Cream

This recipe comes from the kitchen of Chef Edgar Steele of Café Atlantico. It is a fantastic dessert that takes fried ice cream to a new and inventive level. The cinnamon-apple flavor works perfectly with the vanilla ice cream. It's one of the more difficult in this book, but is definitely worth all the effort!

MAKES
4 SERVINGS

▨ VEGETARIAN

FOR THE APPLE CARAMEL

1 cup apple juice

1 cup granulated sugar

Pinch salt

FOR THE CARAMELIZED APPLES

2 tablespoons maple syrup

¼ cinnamon stick

2 Granny Smith apples, peeled, cored, and diced into ½-inch cubes

Pinch salt

FOR THE APPLE CARAMEL

1. In a small saucepan, combine 1 tablespoon of the apple juice and the sugar and heat over medium-low heat. Cook, stirring constantly, until the mixture begins to turn golden in color and gives off a sweet caramel aroma, 2 to 4 minutes.

2. Add the remaining apple juice, reduce the heat to low, and cook until the liquid is reduced to a syrupy consistency, 6 to 8 minutes more. Mix in the salt and reserve the caramel at room temperature.

FOR THE CARAMELIZED APPLES

1. In a medium saucepan, combine the maple syrup and cinnamon stick and cook over low heat until the mixture reduces and begins to create large bubbles, which seem to climb the sides of the pan, 4 to 7 minutes; when the pan is tilted, the bubbles should not move, and the syrup should smell sweet and caramelized, but not burned. Be very careful with the hot sugar. Add the apples to the syrup and gently toss to coat them. The apples will release liquid, so continue to gently toss them and continue cooking until they are very soft. Add the salt and keep the apples warm.

2 pints vanilla bean ice cream

4 ounces dried apple chips

1½ tablespoons granulated
sugar

2 teaspoons ground cinnamon

2 large eggs, beaten

4 cups vegetable oil, for frying

Whole slices of apple chips,
for garnish

FOR THE FRIED ICE CREAM

1. Use an ice cream scoop to place 8 balls of the ice cream onto a baking sheet. Place the balls in the freezer, and allow them to freeze solid.

2. In a food processor, blend the apple chips until they are a coarse-textured powder. In a medium bowl, combine the pulverized chips with the sugar and the cinnamon. Roll the frozen ice cream balls in the mixture, then place back them into the freezer to harden again.

3. In a medium-sized bowl, beat the eggs. Coat the ice cream balls with the egg and then roll them in the apple-chip mixture again. Return the balls to the freezer to harden once again.

4. In a large saucepan, heat the oil to 350°F. Place the ice cream balls, one at a time, into the hot oil. Fry for 1 minute, turning them so that they cook evenly. At this point, the outer crust will be set and crunchy, and the ice cream will be starting to melt.

5. Place some of the caramelized apples on each plate and place 2 balls of ice cream on top. Drizzle some of the apple caramel over the ice cream and garnish with a whole slice of apple chip. Serve immediately.

Mango Sherbet

I like to use skim milk to cut calories when I make this.

MAKES
6 SERVINGS

■ VEGETARIAN

2 cups granulated sugar

1 cup water

½ cup corn syrup

3 cups diced mango

2 cups heavy cream (can use skim milk or 2% milk)

1 tablespoon fresh lemon juice

Mint leaves, for garnish

1. In a small saucepan, combine the sugar, water, and corn syrup and cook over medium heat, stirring constantly, until a simple syrup forms, about 5 minutes.

2. Pour the syrup into a blender and add the mango, cream, and lemon juice and puree until smooth.

3. Pour the mixture into an ice cream maker and follow the manufacturer's instructions. Serve with mint leaves.

4. Store in an airtight container in the freezer for up to 1 month.

Sweet Baked Plantains
with Vanilla Bean Ice Cream

Super easy to make so delicious—this five-star dessert is also naturally gluten-free! Pick plantains that are still a bright greenish yellow color; you want them to be firm for slicing.

MAKES
4 SERVINGS

■ VEGETARIAN

4 semi-ripe plantains

¼ cup packed light brown sugar

1 cup caramel sauce

1 cup hot fudge sauce

1 pint vanilla bean ice cream

1. Preheat the oven to 450°F.

2. Prepare a baking sheet by lining it with parchment paper. Slice the plantains in half lengthwise. Pour the sugar into a shallow dish and roll the plantains in it until they are well coated. Lay the plantains on the baking sheet. Bake for 10 to 12 minutes, or until the sugar has caramelized.

3. Pour the hot fudge and caramel sauces into individual microwave-safe bowls and melt in the microwave, about 30 seconds.

4. Place 1 baked plantain on each plate. Top the plantains with ice cream and drizzle the melted caramel and hot fudge sauces on top. Serve immediately.

Chocolate-Chili-Raspberry Torte

I love chocolate, but sometimes, chocolate desserts can be overwhelming. Here raspberries and orange liqueur offset the richness and chili powder gives it a zing!

MAKES
12 SERVINGS

▨ VEGETARIAN

FOR THE TORTE

2 cups bittersweet chocolate

8 tablespoons unsalted butter

2 cups fresh raspberries

1 tablespoon light brown sugar

1 tablespoon water

5 large eggs

1 cup granulated sugar

1 cup heavy cream

FOR THE TORTE

1. Preheat the oven to 350°F. Grease a 9-inch cake pan with nonstick cooking spray.

2. Melt the chocolate in the top of a double boiler or in a bowl set over a pan of simmering water. Once the chocolate is melted, stir in the butter. Set aside.

3. In a food processor, puree the raspberries with the brown sugar and water.

4. Using a stand mixer, combine the raspberry puree, eggs, granulated sugar, and cream. Beat on high speed until the mixture has doubled in volume.

5. With the mixer on slow speed, fold in the melted chocolate. Pour the batter into the prepared cake pan.

6. Place the cake pan in a large roasting pan. Carefully add water to the larger pan to come halfway up the sides of the cake pan. Bake for 35 minutes. Remove from the oven, transfer to a cooling rack to cool for 45 minutes, then chill for 2 hours in the refrigerator.

7. Once chilled, remove the torte from the pan and place on a serving plate.

FOR THE TOPPING

2 cups pureed fresh
  raspberries

1 cup granulated sugar

⅓ cup heavy cream

¼ cup orange liqueur

¼ cup water

1 tablespoon chili powder,
  or to taste

FOR THE TOPPING

1. In a medium saucepan, combine the pureed raspberries, sugar, cream, liqueur, water, and chili powder. Cook over medium heat, stirring occasionally, until a thick sauce forms, about 20 minutes. Remove from the heat and chill in the refrigerator for about 1 hour. Pour over the torte before serving.

Cinnamon Ice Cream Sandwich

Homemade ice cream is fantastic because you get to choose exactly what you want in it. This recipe makes a basic cinnamon ice cream. For a bolder flavor, try adding pecans, chocolate chips, or caramel sauce.

MAKES
4 SERVINGS

■ VEGETARIAN

1 cup granulated sugar

1 cup heavy cream

1 cup skim milk

1 tablespoon vanilla extract

¼ cup ground cinnamon

1 cup vegetable oil, for frying

8 corn tortillas

Cinnamon sugar (½ cup sugar plus 1½ tablespoons ground cinnamon)

1 cup chocolate sauce

FOR THE ICE CREAM

1. In a medium saucepan, combine the sugar, cream, milk, vanilla, and cinnamon and cook over medium heat, stirring occasionally, until the sugar is melted, 7 to 8 minutes. Set aside to cool for 1 hour.

2. Pour the mixture into an ice cream maker and follow the manufacturer's instructions.

FOR THE SANDWICH

1. In a large saucepan, heat the oil over medium-high heat; it's ready when you see small bubbles forming in the pan. Carefully add a corn tortilla and fry just until the tortilla stiffens, about 1 minute. Remove the tortilla from the oil and sprinkle with the cinnamon sugar. Repeat with the remaining tortillas.

2. Put a tortilla on each of 4 plates. Place a large scoop of ice cream in the center of each. Cover with chocolate sauce. Top with a second tortilla to complete each sandwich. Serve immediately.

Celiac Disease RESOURCES

American Celiac Disease Alliance

2504 Duxbury Place

Alexandria, VA 22308

Phone: 703-622-3331

E-mail: info@americanceliac.org

Web site: www.americanceliac.org

American Dietetic Association

120 South Riverside Plaza, Suite 2000

Chicago, IL 60606-6995

Phone: 800-877-1600

E-mail: hotline@eatright.org

Web site: www.eatright.org

Celiac Disease Foundation

13251 Ventura Boulevard, #1

Studio City, CA 91604

Phone: 818-990-2354

Fax: 818-990-2379

E-mail: cdf@celiac.org

Web site: www.celiac.org

Celiac Sprue Association/ USA, Inc.

P.O. Box 31700

Omaha, NE 68131-0700

Phone: 877-CSA-4CSA (272-4272)

Fax: 402-643-4108

E-mail: celiacs@csaceliacs.org

Web site: www.csaceliacs.org

Children's Digestive Health and Nutrition Foundation

1501 Bethlehem Pike

P.O. Box 6

Flourtown, PA 19031

Phone: 215-233-0808

Fax: 215-233-3918

E-mail: cdhnf@cdhnf.org

Web site: www.cdhnf.org

Gluten Intolerance Group
of North America

31214 124th Avenue SE

Auburn, WA 98092-3667

Phone: 253-833-6655

Fax: 253-833-6675

E-mail: info@gluten.net

Web site: www.gluten.net

National Foundation for Celiac
Awareness

224 South Maple Street

P.O. Box 544

Ambler, PA 19002-0544

Phone: 215-325-1306

E-mail: info@celiaccentral.org

Web site: www.celiaccentral.org

National Institutes of Health

Celiac Disease Awareness Campaign

c/o National Digestive Diseases
Information Clearinghouse

2 Information Way

Bethesda, MD 20892-3570

Phone: 800-891-5389

Fax: 703-738-4929

E-mail: celiac@info.niddk.nih.gov

Web site: celiac.nih.gov

North American Society for
Pediatric Gastroenterology,
Hepatology and Nutrition

P.O. Box 6

1501 Bethlehem Pike

Flourtown, PA 19031

Phone: 215-233-0808

Fax: 215-233-3918

E-mail: naspghan@naspghan.org

Web site: www.naspghan.org

Prometheus Laboratories Inc.

9410 Carroll Park Drive

San Diego, CA 92121

Phone: 888-423-5227, option 3

Fax: 877-816-4019

Web site: prometheuslabs.com

2G Pharma Inc.

6-2400 Dundas Street West

Suite 724

Mississauga, Ontario

Canada L5K 2K8

Phone: 905-271-2122

E-mail: info@2gpharma.com

Index of DAIRY-FREE RECIPES

Index of
VEGETARIAN RECIPES

INDEX

About the Author

Vanessa Maltin is the food & lifestyle editor of *Delight Gluten-Free Magazine,* a publication geared toward people with food allergies, Celiac Disease, and other medical conditions relating to food. She is also the author of *Beyond Rice Cakes: A Young Person's Guide to Cooking, Eating & Living Gluten-Free.* In addition, she consults for a variety of gluten-free food manufacturers and is an active member of the advisory board of the Celiac Disease Program at Children's National Medical Center, Washington, DC.

Vanessa has appeared on numerous television shows as an expert on gluten-free food and Celiac Disease: Planet Green's *Emeril Green,* CNBC's *On the Money,* and *CNN Newsroom* with Heidi Collins. She writes the Celiac Princess blog (www.celiacprincess.com), which receives thousands of visitors every month.

Vanessa earned a bachelor's degree in journalism from the George Washington University and holds certificates in the Practical Applications of Food Allergy Guidelines and Nutritional Analysis for Federal School Breakfast and Lunch Programs. She is currently a student at the Institute of Culinary Education in New York.

Previously, Vanessa was the director of programming and communications for the National Foundation for Celiac Awareness. In this role she was responsible for such programs as the foundation's Gluten-Free Cooking Sprees, continuing education for medical professionals and chefs, media outreach, and strategic partnerships with corporations. Vanessa was also the editorial director of the NFCA monthly *Celiac-Central* newsletter. In her role as the host of *Alternative Appetites,* a video podcast series, she supports people with Celiac Disease and other special dietary needs in cooking delicious food suitable for their specific conditions. In her spare time Vanessa enjoys cooking, playing the flute, ballroom dancing, and pursuing anything related to increasing the public's awareness of Celiac Disease and gluten-free living.